The Security Economy

OECD

ORGANISATION FOR ECONOMIC CO-OPERATION AND DEVELOPMENT

ORGANISATION FOR ECONOMIC CO-OPERATION AND DEVELOPMENT

Pursuant to Article 1 of the Convention signed in Paris on 14th December 1960, and which came into force on 30th September 1961, the Organisation for Economic Co-operation and Development (OECD) shall promote policies designed:

- to achieve the highest sustainable economic growth and employment and a rising standard of living in member countries, while maintaining financial stability, and thus to contribute to the development of the world economy;
- to contribute to sound economic expansion in member as well as non-member countries in the process of economic development; and
- to contribute to the expansion of world trade on a multilateral, non-discriminatory basis in accordance with international obligations.

The original member countries of the OECD are Austria, Belgium, Canada, Denmark, France, Germany, Greece, Iceland, Ireland, Italy, Luxembourg, the Netherlands, Norway, Portugal, Spain, Sweden, Switzerland, Turkey, the United Kingdom and the United States. The following countries became members subsequently through accession at the dates indicated hereafter: Japan (28th April 1964), Finland (28th January 1969), Australia (7th June 1971), New Zealand (29th May 1973), Mexico (18th May 1994), the Czech Republic (21st December 1995), Hungary (7th May 1996), Poland (22nd November 1996), Korea (12th December 1996) and the Slovak Republic (14th December 2000). The Commission of the European Communities takes part in the work of the OECD (Article 13 of the OECD Convention).

Publié en français sous le titre :
L'Économie de la sécurité

Foreword

The security industry is a large and expanding area of economic activity. Spurred on by the perception of rising crime, the threat of terrorist attacks and increasingly free movements of goods, capital and people, there has been a swell in government, corporate and consumers' budgets for security goods and services in recent years. This development promises to have far-reaching economic and societal implications over the longer term. The challenge for policy makers is how to meet the apparent need for greater security without unduly impeding economic efficiency and citizens' rights in liberal societies.

In mid-2003, I spoke with a number of senior officials of OECD member countries about exploring the phenomenon of the "new security economy". It was clear to me that the overall concept was not fully understood, as it was really a convergence of new trends in our societies. Ever higher performance technologies are providing tools for new goods and services in our economies, including the monitoring, storing and instant retrieval of large data and information sets. Larger relational databases linked to computational capacity are creating new possibilities for the tracking and control of information about goods and services – and about people and the global environment itself. Equally clearly, national security issues were likely to prove an important factor in focusing the interest of governments and the private sector. What we wanted to do in the International Futures Programme was to offer a platform to discuss the future of the security economy, its components and its drivers, both in the private and in the public sector.

A first step was to develop a framework for the concept itself. To provide the necessary input at an early stage, we produced a scoping document defining and outlining the type of issues that were emerging from this convergence of technologies and new security needs. We then proceeded with the design of the Forum meeting itself, on the basis of which we invited the presentations and papers. We held the Forum on December 8, 2003 in the Paris Headquarters of the OECD.

The meeting consisted of four sessions. The first reviewed the social, economic and institutional drivers behind the rising demand for security and sketched out the trends and developments likely to determine its future scale and direction. The second session looked at the supply side, outlining the state of the art in several key technologies in identification, authentication and surveillance and exploring their likely development over the next ten years or so. The third examined the longer-term economic implications of the emerging security economy. It addressed key trade-offs in the coming years between greater security on the one hand and economic efficiency on the other, and explored the roles that governments and the private sector might play in helping to resolve these trade-offs. The fourth and final session considered the mid- to long-term implications for society of the growing use of security technologies. More specifically, it was about the future of the "surveillance society" and what can be done to guide the development and utilisation of identification and monitoring technologies along avenues that society regards, on balance, as generally most beneficial.

Barrie Stevens designed and organised the meeting, and contributed the report's first two chapters. Jack Radisch conducted the initial scoping of the concept and issues. Research assistance was provided by Marit Undseth, and logistical support by Concetta Miano. Randall Holden edited this volume.

The book is published under the responsibility of the Secretary-General of the OECD.

Michael W. Oborne
Director,
Multi-Disciplinary Issues,
OECD International Futures Programme

THE SECURITY ECONOMY – ISBN 92-64-10772-X – © OECD 2004

Table of Contents

ISBN 92-64-10772-X
The Security Economy
OECD 2004

Chapter 1

The Emerging Security Economy:
An Introduction

by

Barrie Stevens
OECD Secretariat, Advisory Unit to the Secretary-General

"Security" has become a very prominent issue in recent years. Faced with an array of potential hazards, from terrorism and computer viruses to fraud and organised crime, the world is perceived by many to be an increasingly dangerous place. As a result, the focus on security issues has sharpened and the demand for security-related goods and services has steadily grown, giving rise to a wide and varied range of economic activities in both the government domain and the business sector. This is the emerging security economy.

The term "security economy" is, like the concept it denotes, relatively new. It attempts to describe a kaleidoscope cluster of activities concerned with preventing or reducing risk of deliberate harm to life and property. At the broadest level, it could include all matters related to defence and counter-intelligence, the public police force, private policing, armed guards, and security technology providers. In a much narrower sense, it might comprise just private spending on personal and corporate security. For the purposes of this publication, the security economy is considered to comprise principally the security industry, including its interfaces with security-related activities of governments and their agencies.

The security industry is the aggregation of hundreds of thousands of businesses and individuals whose aim is to sell safety from malevolent acts threatening life, property and other assets, and information. The products and services generated range from fire and burglar alarms, locks and safes, through electronic access control and biometrics, electronic article surveillance and security consulting, to armoured car services, guard equipment and security fencing. For a long time the security industry operated – to a large extent, at least – separately from public law enforcement and military charged with national security. However, in recent years the industry seems to be increasingly overlapping with these other actors. Security companies used to sell the bulk of their goods and services to homes and businesses; now government has become an important customer, and moreover has acted to strengthen security regulations that affect private actors in several other industries. Not surprisingly perhaps, it is argued in some quarters that the time is not ripe to talk of a "security industry" given its high degree of diversity and fragmentation and lack of truly unifying points of interface with customers. In other quarters, however, there is a feeling that, even if there is as yet no clearly definable security industry, there most likely will be in the not-too-distant future. Such divergence of views is not unusual around an important "emerging" industry.

Even at a relatively restricted level of definition, the security economy is not easy to quantify. Not all security measures translate into expenditures, making them difficult to evaluate. Moreover, in many cases it is difficult to measure any value added to security because it is increasingly embedded in a multitude of goods and services. In addition, sound data on spending on security are hard to come by, and estimates are often highly approximative. Thus for the most part, assessments of the size of the private security industry and the extent of its development over time have to rely on trade associations' material and specialised consultancy reports. Information about public sector spending on security is available for a few countries, but it suffers from the same delineation problems as private spending on security.

Despite these difficulties of measurement, the indications are that the security industry is emerging as a big player in the economy, and expanding. Available estimates put the private security industry's turnover at between USD 100 billion and USD 120 billion worldwide. The largest share is accounted for by the United States, although other OECD countries have sizeable security industries as well. For example, Germany's is thought to be around USD 4 billion and France's and the United Kingdom's around USD 3 billion. While there is little evidence within the industry of a major upsurge in spending on security since September 11, 2001, longer-term data suggest healthy growth in turnover in the order of 7-8% annually, easily outstripping average annual economic growth rates.

Key factors shaping demand

What is driving such rapid expansion? Growth in global demand for security goods and services is being powered to some degree by technological progress. But, as Chapter 2 of this book highlights, the principal drivers are a wide and diverse range of social, economic and institutional factors.

Many have to do with a demand at all levels – government, businesses and individuals – for increased prevention and detection of and protection against criminal acts such as fraud and the dealings of the underground economy, theft and vandalism as well as drug-related offences and violent crimes. Interestingly, statistics on recorded crimes indicate that in many countries ordinary (as opposed to organised) crime rates have in fact been diminishing since the mid-1990s. Organised crime, on the other hand, has grown in many countries. This suggests that the overall picture of crime trends is in fact quite mixed. It also suggests that people's perceptions of levels of criminal activity are a very important ingredient of their sense of insecurity and that – such being the case – technology is not always a solution.

Notwithstanding the fact that some categories of crime in some countries are diminishing, the overall burden of crime on the economy appears to be huge. Recent attempts to quantify its cost at national level estimate it to be the equivalent of 20% of GDP in the United States and around 7% of GDP in the United Kingdom. The measure includes not only real costs in the form of financial outlays for crime prevention and prisons, but also intangible costs such as physical injury and mental stress.

The potential for large-scale damage from acts of terrorism and the threat from weapons of mass effect, especially after the events of September 11, have also emerged as significant factors underpinning the growing demand for security.

Globalisation has become a further important driver behind security concerns. For example, expanding foreign trade stimulates increased transport of people and cargo. Growth in air, rail, road and maritime transport increases the risk of security breaches that facilitate robbery and organised smuggling, thereby lending impetus to governments' efforts to tighten cross-border surveillance. Rising immigration weakens countries' ability to impede clandestine threats, while fuelling in some cases communities' sense of insecurity. The growing internationalisation of production activities has seen communications and supply chains become increasingly global, specialised and fragmented, giving rise to particular vulnerabilities. At the same time businesses and governments are seeking ways of conducting their operations more efficiently and managing security more cost-effectively. In some cases – the creation of the US Department for Homeland Security is a striking example – institutional restructuring has helped boost demand. And new and ever more sophisticated surveillance and authentication technologies continue to come on stream at ever more affordable prices.

Projections and forecasts from various sources suggest that these drivers will continue to stimulate security-related activities in the years to come. Rising mobility is set to pose particular security and efficiency challenges to governments and the business community alike. World merchandise is expected to continue to outpace economic growth rates over the medium term, associated with high expansion rates in a number of transport sectors such as air cargo. Similarly, it is anticipated that migration pressures will persist throughout the next decades. For example, the UN projects an average annual net flow of migrants of over 1 million to the United States, over 200 000 to Germany and over 170 000 to Canada. The growing momentum of e-commerce will meanwhile offer ample scope for cyber-crime. Finally, questions remain – especially with regard to OECD countries – as to the future impact of ageing societies on general perceptions of risk and the demand for security goods and services.

Tomorrow's identification and surveillance technologies

Against the backdrop of an overall expansion of security activity, the technologies employed to carry out security functions have also benefited from substantial growth. Monitoring and identification products, for example, are currently thought to be a USD 15 billion market. These are products that make up the "backbone" of corporate security systems and include access control, perimeter control and biometrics. Computer security products are currently considered a USD 4 billion market and include tokens, cards and biometrics for providing "front-end" security to verify individuals' access. Growth projections over the next 7-10 years are also very healthy. In global terms, the security industry is expected to maintain its historical growth rates of 7-8% p.a., but prospects for some segments are particularly favourable – not least biometrics, radio frequency identification (RFID) technologies and computer security.

Indeed, RFID and biometrics are among the technologies that have come to the fore in recent years and are expected to play a key role in security in the future; others include satellite-based navigation and tracking, encryption, and advances in telecommunications. Moreover, some of the more established surveillance technologies have gained prominence as they have merged with ICT technologies – closed circuit television (CCTV) is a striking example.

Biometrics

Since the late 1990s, biometrics has become an increasingly viable solution for securing access to premises, computers and networks. Digital scanning – of the finger, face, iris, retina, voice, etc. – is already used in applications ranging from citizen ID and network access to surveillance and telephony. In the future these applications are expected to expand quite rapidly, and as Bernard Didier points out in Chapter 3 of this publication, significant efforts are likely to be put into raising their performance, for example by improving techniques for detecting biometric artefacts (false fingers, false iris, etc.); for developing surveillance by remote identification; and so on. However, effective solutions will need to be found if potential obstacles to public acceptance – resistance to fingerprinting, privacy concerns, etc. – are to be overcome.

Radio frequency identification systems

RFID technologies have gained considerably in popularity in recent years. Commerce in particular uses technologies such as tracking devices and smart labels embedded with transmitting sensors and intelligent readers to convey information about the location of merchandise and consumer behaviour. Various systems are in use – electronic article surveillance (EAS), portable data capture, networked systems and positioning systems – albeit on a fairly small scale, since RFID technology is still too expensive to be used en mass, *e.g.* by retailers. The next few years are likely to see a broad range of pilot schemes applied to a variety of uses – for instance, the tracking of apparel, hazardous goods, consumer packaged goods, currency, and medical patients. In Chapter 4, Steve Hodges and Duncan McFarlane also point to potential uses for RFID in "checkout free" retail stores, in the home for monitoring inventories, and for providing information about products as they move through the supply chain. A number of obstacles will have to be overcome, however, not least the high investment costs in setting up RFID systems and the thorny issue of privacy.

Satellite-based tracking and surveillance

As René Oosterlinck shows in Chapter 5, the applications for these technologies have expanded significantly in recent years. They are currently used for a multitude of related functions, ranging from navigation technologies for maritime traffic and private automobiles to the observation of shipping movements and land transport of goods, vehicle-fleet management, and the monitoring of vehicles for the purposes of road use charging. As more satellites are launched and highly sophisticated satellite systems such as Galileo become operational later this decade, current uses are set to expand and new applications are likely to emerge.

"Hybrid technology" cards

Highly sophisticated optical memory cards with embedded holograms for rapid visual authentication are now coming into use, often containing micro image security features and multi-application IC chips that provide access to (for instance) e-government services. In Chapter 6, Alfio Torrisi and Luigi Mezzanotte demonstrate how such technologies are being employed in Italy's drive to provide all its citizens with a secure electronic ID card within the next five years.

In sum, the crucial element in the growth of security technologies over the medium- to long-term future is unlikely to be technological, but rather the degree of public acceptance that these technologies encounter, whether their benefits are clearly recognised, and the priority that consumers accord their security concerns.

The longer-term economic implications

As events of recent years have demonstrated, the security threats to local, national and regional economies are many and diverse. Above all, they can exact a heavy price. It is now thought that, quite apart from the tragic loss of human life, the economic cost of the terrorist attacks on September 11 totalled around USD 120 billion. This includes not only the impact on physical assets and infrastructures but also that on employment, financial markets, business continuity and so on. Subsequently, major industries have begun to address the issue of large-scale threats to their own business. For example, the maritime transport industry considers that a well-co-ordinated terrorist attack on its system would cause losses running into tens of billions of US dollars. However, less dramatic felonies can also be very expensive. By way of illustration, in the United States the cost of fraud in entitlement benefits alone was estimated at USD 750 million in the late 1990s; identity theft is thought to cost banks and other credit institutions about USD 2 billion annually. Over two-fifths of all UK firms have recently reported security breaches, suggesting losses to the business community as a whole in the order of several billion pounds.

Improving security, however, also comes at a price, of which there are generally two types: first, the investment required to put in place the requisite security arrangements, and second, the negative impact the security arrangements may have on the operations of the sector or the entire economy.

Faced with huge potential losses from serious threats, governments and businesses are forced to consider potentially huge investments. Following up on the above example from the maritime transport sector, it is thought that the initial burden on ship operators imposed by the security actions negotiated at the International Maritime Organisation could be in the order of well over USD 600 million. Businesses almost everywhere are investing more in protecting their assets and their information systems. Estimates for the United States, for instance, suggest that the total homeland security cost for the private sector resulting from the September 11 attacks will be about USD 10 billion a year, although initially [i.e. 2003] they could be much higher – in the range of USD 46 billion to USD 76 billion. Governments and other public authorities have also increased their overall spending on security, in some cases quite substantially. The US Homeland Security budget doubled from fiscal 2002/03 to its current level of well over USD 30 billion: funding for aviation security is now running at USD 4.8 billion and for border security at USD 10.6 billion. Whether such investments are funded by government taxes or private spending, their imprint on the economy is not insignificant.

Tighter security may also mean longer delivery times and disruption of global supply chains and of finely-tuned just-in-time delivery systems. As a result of increased security concerns in recent years, trading companies have been confronted with additional costs relating to transport, handling, insurance and customs. These "frictional" costs tend to make trade more expensive and reduce flows. According to OECD simulations, measures introduced in the wake of September 11 could increase trading costs by 1%, leading to global welfare losses of around USD 75 billion per year.

There are other potential trade-offs, as Tilman Brück points out in Chapter 7 of this book – for example, between security and globalisation, and security and technological progress. And there are other significant indirect and second-order effects from insecurity, many of which are poorly understood and difficult to quantify.

Of course, these factors have to be put in perspective. The costs may be high in the short and medium term, but to the extent that they prevent serious damage and disruption, the long-term benefits can be enormous. The question is how to achieve the optimal balance between security measures and efficiency. New technologies may help, and the literature has an abundant supply of case studies and illustrations. One study of a new electronic manifest handling system proposed by American Customs has estimated the direct savings to US importers alone to be over USD 22 billion over 20 years, and savings to the US Government to be well over USD 4 billion over the same period.

However, there is also scope for reassessing the respective roles of the public and private sectors. The main argument for justifying government intervention is the public-good nature of security. Agents do not necessarily take into account the positive externality their investment in security has on others. As a result, the actual level of security tends to be suboptimal. Such undesirable outcomes can be mitigated by regulation or by co-ordination coupled with credible enforcement rules. But the question remains as to the extent to which governments should be involved, how they should intervene, and which policies deserve priority.

Given the negative externalities linked to major disasters, there may be some room for government subsidies to assist the private sector with improving security, provided the familiar subsidy pitfalls are avoided. Where government regulation appears the most appropriate tool, the involvement of the affected businesses is essential. Indeed, the last few years have seen much more responsibility for security imposed on the operators of airlines, financial institutions and so on. This has often left private sector actors feeling that risks are being increasingly transferred to the private sector, imposing costs on companies that can be significant but not always visible. However, even where there may be a strong case for shifting the burden of security costs between public and private bearers of risk, difficult choices have to be made about the tool to be used, e.g. tax or regulation. Clearly, more thought will need to be given to tailoring government policies affecting the security economy to prevailing conditions and preferences.

There would appear to be substantial potential for public-private co-operation in the security field, not least for voluntary private-sector schemes backed by government action. These may take, for example, the nature of initiatives to ensure the integrity of entire supply chains through agreements among shippers, intermediaries and carriers, with governments acting both as active partners to the agreement (*e.g.* customs and immigration) and as facilitators (*e.g.* outsourcing assurance, validation and certification to accredited private-sector operations).

Longer-term societal implications

With the spread and increasing sophistication of security technologies, a number of developments are occurring simultaneously. To begin with, surveillance is becoming increasingly *intense*. It is also becoming more *privatised*: in the United States, for example, expenditures on private security are estimated to be more than twice those on public law enforcement, after having grown more than fivefold over the two decades between 1980 and 2000. Moreover, security technologies are ever more *automated*, increasingly *integrated* with databases containing personal information, and also increasingly *globalised*.

The chapters mentioned above document the rising use of surveillance technologies and suggest that there will be considerable growth in this area in the future. The enhanced effectiveness of the technologies is being brought about, at least in part, by linking them to searchable databases and using high-performance computing technologies to check, sort and identify. A case in point is CCTV coupled with facial recognition facilities that are algorithmic (or mathematically coded) to enable computers to sort and categorise on the basis of facial features, expressions or behavioural patterns. Thus, as David Lyon points out in Chapter 8 of this publication, in the 21st century these processes of "social sorting" and "discrimination" are becoming increasingly automated. Interestingly, it is not just in the area of law enforcement and government administration that such sorting techniques have developed, but also in marketing. Hence, surveillance practices cluster people (often without their knowledge) into categories, be it as potential lawbreakers or as potential consumers. The upshot is a rise in the use of risk profiling and increasing reliance on "predictive profiling".

At the same time, in settings both public and private, state and civil, surveillance practices are converging and databases from various sources – public services, police, intelligence, business, consumers – look set to become increasingly integrated. And as public and commercial data networks intermesh, the potential for global surveillance (at airports and ports, through data collection by multinational corporations, etc.) is considerably heightened.

Important questions thus arise relating to how society as a whole will choose to respond to the spread of surveillance and identification technologies in the years to come. For example, until now security and democratic liberties have tended to be seen as alternatives rather than as possibly complementary notions. Issues of privacy are important, but equally important for the future are those of accountability. How are surveillance and monitoring systems controlled? Who creates the categories? What are the consequences of social sorting and risk profiling for ordinary people? And will government continue to be considered the key institution for regulation when in fact numerous opportunities exist for local organisations and agencies to regulate themselves within an established legal framework?

Not all the signs for the future are negative. Some organisations are indeed taking much more care with personal, sensitive information; awareness of the vulnerability of personal data is growing; and recently international agreements have begun to emerge which place much tighter constraints on the kinds of personal data permitted to cross borders. The advance of identification and surveillance technologies seems to many to be unstoppable; and perhaps the most that can be done is to guide their development and utilisation along avenues that society regards as generally the most beneficial. What will be crucial is the interplay between the technologies in question, society's assessment of their pros and cons, and the regulator's response.

ISBN 92-64-10772-X
The Security Economy
OECD 2004

Chapter 2

Factors Shaping Future Demand for Security Goods and Services

by

Barrie Stevens
OECD Secretariat, Advisory Unit to the Secretary-General

The security sector is emerging as a big player in the economy, and is expanding fast. It is made up of hundreds of thousands of businesses and individuals essentially selling *safety* – the means to protect life, property and other assets, and information. The products and services it produces range from the simplest fire and burglar alarms to the most sophisticated biometric devices. Estimates put the industry's turnover at over USD 100 billion. The lion's share is accounted for by the United States, but other OECD countries have a large security sector, too – for example, turnover is thought to be around USD 4 billion in Germany and USD 3 billion in France and the United Kingdom. Historical growth rates for the industry average 7-8% worldwide, outpacing economic growth rates by a considerable margin.

This remarkable expansion of the security industry's activities is being shaped by a wide and diverse range of social, economic and institutional factors. Crime – real and perceived – and the desire to prevent it and protect from it play an important role. So too, in recent years, does fear of the consequences of terrorist acts. Equally, broader economic forces are at work. Globalisation is intensifying the movement of people, goods and services across the world, bringing to many not only greater prosperity but also heightened risks of smuggling, theft, drug trafficking, counterfeiting, illegal entry, disruption to global supply networks, and so on. At the same time, businesses and governments are seeking ways of conducting their operations more efficiently and managing security more cost-effectively, while new and ever more sophisticated surveillance and authentication technologies come on stream at ever more affordable prices.

This chapter endeavours to provide a somewhat more systematic overview of these factors and to explore their significance as drivers of future demand for security goods and services. The projections cited here are not intended to predict the future but merely to communicate a sense of how, in the years to come, many of the factors likely to determine the security environment may grow in significance.

1. Growing preoccupation with criminal activity

The aggregate burden of crime on the economy is huge, by any standards. Recent studies quantify the cost at national level to be around 20% of GDP in the United States and 7% of GDP in the United Kingdom. These estimates include real costs in the form of spending on crime prevention and prisons, and also intangible costs such as physical injuries sustained and mental stress.

Three issues stand out in the relationship between trends in crime and demand for security goods and services. First, insecurity is an integral part of human nature, and the need for security therefore highly subjective. For many people, no amount of prevention or protection will calm their fundamental anxiety. Second, it follows from this that people's *perceptions* of crime, its incidence and its seriousness, are likely to be just as important as actual crime levels. And third, while reported crime rates in most OECD countries in recent years reveal broad common trends, some developments remain uneven both among countries and across categories of crime.

A *priori*, one could suspect a robust link between ordinary (as opposed to organised) crime rates on the one hand and demand for security goods and services on the other. At the aggregate level, however, the relationship is far from simple, and movements in overall levels of crime do not appear to be a satisfactory indicator of general trends in security spending. As mentioned above, markets for security goods and services have been expanding very rapidly, yet in several OECD countries trends in recorded crime peaked in the early 1990s (after rising quite significantly in the 1980s) and drifted downwards thereafter.

Figure 1. **Trends in reported crime levels in selected OECD countries, 1993-2002**

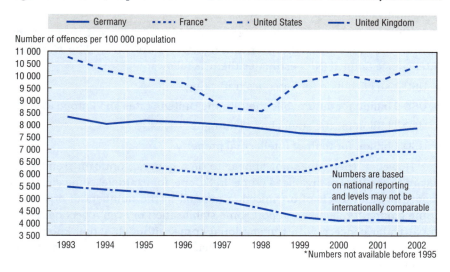

Source: OECD, derived from Interpol, 2003.

More detailed breakdowns of crime data do occasionally provide interesting pointers that serve to underpin the relationship in question. Aggregate figures for the United States, for example, show a fall in all categories of offences since the early/mid-1990s, including burglary. Yet a breakdown by location indicates that residential robberies have actually increased over the period. This may help explain the growing use of video surveillance, alarms and other security systems in US homes despite the decline in crime rates more generally.

It could of course also be argued – given the complexities of crime statistics and the well-known problems of over- and under-reporting, divergencies between reported and recorded offences, and so on – that official statistics do not reflect ordinary citizens' perceptions of insecurity in the face of growing urban violence, drug-related offences, and various other crimes. However, this is not always borne out by household surveys. The British Crime Survey, for example, monitors trends in "worry" about various kinds of offences – burglary, muggings, rape – and individuals' assessments of their personal safety. On the whole, these survey trends tend to reflect quite closely the general decline in crime rates recorded through the 1990s.

As for the future, one can only speculate as to the effect of broader socioeconomic developments on crime levels and the way citizens will perceive them. Will rising incomes lead to a lower incidence of crimes? Will the growing proportion of elderly in OECD populations change society's attitudes to security in fundamental ways (leading for example to more gated residencies and cities)?

With respect to organised crime, available data suggest that current annual revenues from illicit criminal activity are huge. The National Intelligence Council (NIC) estimates them as follows:

- USD 100-300 billion for narcotics trafficking.
- USD 9 billion for automobile theft (in the United States and Europe alone).
- USD 7 billion for the smuggling of humans.
- USD 1 billion for theft of intellectual property.

However, there does not appear to be a general, uniform trend with regard to the level of organised crime. In Europe, for example, some countries report a rise in levels of organised crime and in the numbers of organised crime groups, while others report some stabilisation or even a decline. There is particular concern with transnational crime; although actual knowledge remains disparate, there are indications that it is on the rise. Increasing cross-border co-operation among criminal organisations stems in part from the growing interdependence of national economies and flows of cross-border traffic of people and goods, as noted above. As globalisation gathers pace in the future, so too will the opportunities for transnational crime.

2. Changing patterns of terrorist activity

Forms of terrorism have emerged in recent years which differ in important respects from what might be called "traditional" terrorism. The goal of terrorists is often sustained opposition to an entire economic, social, political or cultural system; they have acquired a more global dimension; and – as the events of September 11, 2001, Bali, Istanbul, etc. have shown – their attacks often aim to kill as many civilians as possible, an accentuation of a trend that began in the 1980s. It has been observed, for instance, that while the number of transborder terrorist attacks fell between the 1980s and 1990s by nearly 60%, the number of fatalities and other casualties caused by such acts increased by 20%.

Thus, places where people gather in large numbers such as metro and railway stations, shopping malls and large buildings have become natural targets. Moreover, the more recent forms of terrorism also try to take advantage of modern societies' reliance on critical infrastructures such as energy, water, transport, healthcare, financial services and information systems. Destruction or at least lengthy disruption of such infrastructures may entail a heavy human and economic cost. Hence, protecting public places and vital systems has become a priority task not only for governments but also for the operators of critically important facilities, and this in turn has boosted surveillance, prevention and protection services.

3. The growing mobility of people and goods

The globalisation process of recent decades has been propelled to a large degree by the growth of transport and communications at all levels – local, regional, national and international.

The rapid and sustained rise in the movements of people and merchandise worldwide has spurred economic activity and contributed significantly to the rising levels of prosperity experienced by many societies. The flip side of the coin, however, is that those same channels are vulnerable to abuse through theft, fraud, the trafficking of humans and animals, terrorist operations and so on, putting increasing pressure on governments and businesses to monitor such movements more closely.

a) Mobility of people

Passenger travel in all its forms has expanded enormously, propelled on the demand side by economic growth, higher disposable incomes and increased leisure time, and on the supply side by falling transportation prices and technological change.

Figure 2. **Motor vehicle kilometres traveled (VKT), 1990 to 2020**

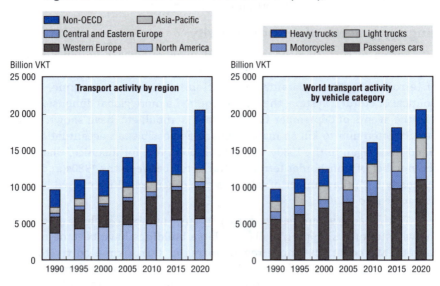

Source: OECD Environmental Outlook, 2001.

As Figure 2 above highlights, passenger traffic on roads has undergone a remarkable expansion. Other forms of passenger transport, however, have also grown. Air passenger traffic for instance has seen particularly rapid growth, expanding at an average annual rate of 9% since 1960. This sector is expected to continue growing in the future, albeit at somewhat lower rates. Aircraft manufacturers such as Airbus see world annual traffic more than doubling between today and 2020, driven largely by rising incomes, higher carrier efficiency and lower fares (Figure 3).

The highest growth in international air passenger traffic is expected within the Asian region, where inter-regional flights are expected to expand rapidly, and between Asia and North America and Asia and Europe. Intra-European passenger traffic is also set to grow rapidly as economic integration deepens and widens with the accession of new EU member states (Figure 4). These trends are an indication of the pressures that governments, agencies, carriers and airport operators will face in the coming years as they strive to process the growing volumes of cross-border passenger traffic.

International migration is part of this overall picture. Inflows of foreigners into OECD countries began to rise in the mid-1980s, peaked in the early 1990s, declined, and then picked up again in the late 1990s (Figure 5). This more recent upturn confirmed the increasing role of migration in

Figure 3. **Air passenger traffic projections: growth in air traffic 2000-2020**

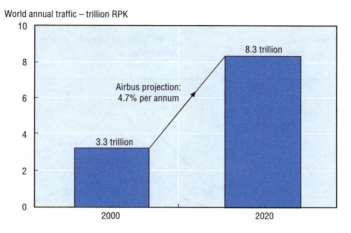

Source: OECD.

Figure 4. **Air passenger traffic projections: top ten markets**

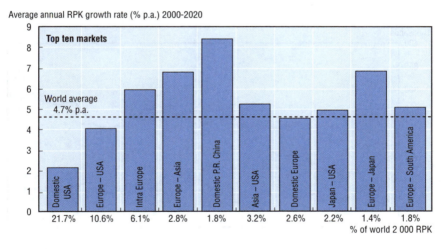

Source: Airbus.

economic globalisation. In the past decade geopolitical changes, notably greater freedom of movement in Central and Eastern Europe, have enlarged the scope for international migration, and an increasing number of immigrants from Asia, sub-Saharan Africa and Central and Latin America

Figure 5. **Inward migration into selected OECD countries 1980-2000**

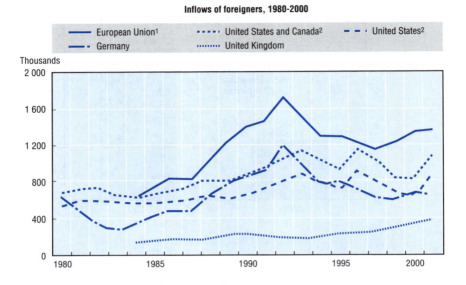

Inflows of foreigners, 1980-2000

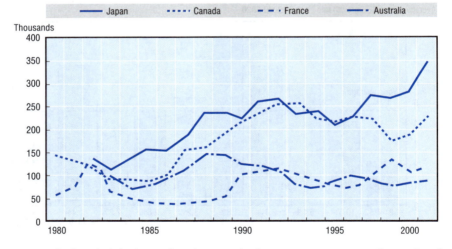

Note: Data for the United Kingdom are from the International Passenger Survey. For Australia, Canada and the United States, data relate to new permanent immigrants; for France and South European countries, data are issued from residence permits. For all other countries, data are based on Population Registers.

1. Belgium, Denmark, Germany, France, Luxembourg, the Netherlands, Sweden, and the United Kingdom.

2. Excluding immigrants legalised in the United States under IRCA regularisation programme.

Source: OECD, 2002.

have added impetus to flows toward several OECD countries. Over 2000-01, inflows continued to grow, especially to the United States, Canada, Australia, Japan, the United Kingdom and southern Europe. Much was related to employment and, particularly for asylum flows, to family reunions. Illegal immigration has also persisted.

A complex set of factors are at work which will likely ensure that the pressures behind migratory inflows into OECD countries continue at least into the next few decades: huge gaps between industrialised and developing countries in living standards and in birth rates; ageing populations and shrinking labour forces in many of the developed economies; the relatively low cost of transport and communication; the presence of migratory networks; environmental degradation, wars and civil strife; and in some countries, the collapse of governance. Not surprisingly therefore, various projections expect OECD countries to remain net receivers of around 2 million migrants per year on average through the first half of the 21st century. Among the largest net gainers are likely to be the United States (over 1 million per year), Germany (173 000), Canada (136 000) and Australia (83 000).

Given these prospects, and the fact that not all OECD societies readily welcome migrants, countries face an enormous task of maintaining effective and efficient controls at ports, airports and other border crossings in the coming years.

Figure 6. **Major migration patterns in the early 21st century**

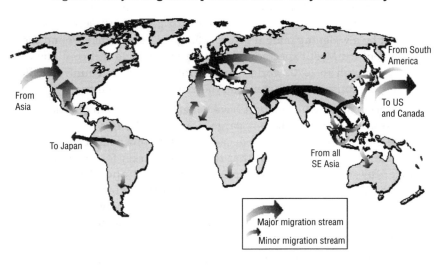

Source: Population Reference Bureau, *International Migration: Facing the Challenge*, March 2002.

Figure 7. **World exports, 1995-2020**

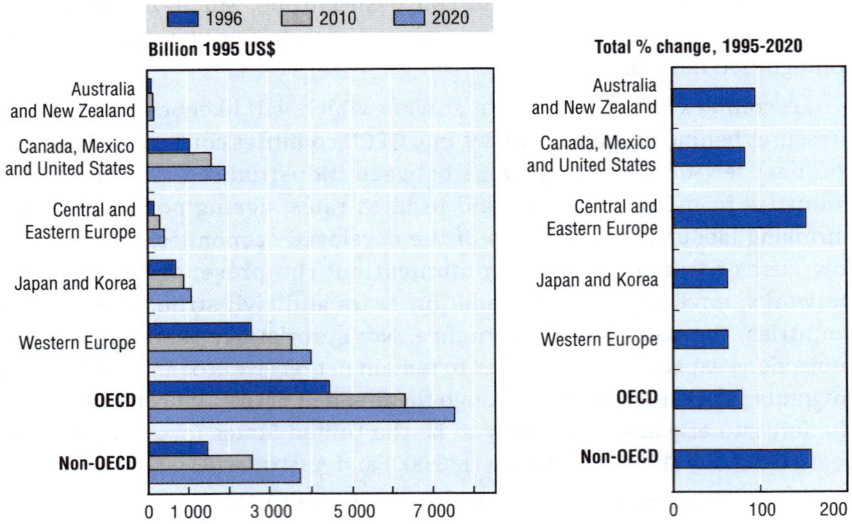

Source: OECD Environmental Outlook, 2001.

b) Mobility of goods

A useful indication of the growing mobility of merchandise is international trade. World trade grew at an annual average of 4% between 1980 and 1993 and then surged to 8% per annum over the period 1994-96, outpacing world output by a widening margin before falling back somewhat around the turn of the century. Most expectations are that world trade will continue to grow apace through to 2020; world exports from non-OECD countries will most likely grow considerably faster than those from OECD countries.

Some forms of freight transport have benefited more than others from the expansion of world trade. Air cargo, for example, has experienced remarkable growth in the past few decades, and its prospects continue to be favourable. Projections suggest that the global market for merchandise transported by air could easily triple between 2001 and 2020. Above-average growth in air cargo is expected for intra-Asian, Asia-North America, and Europe-Asia routes. Other means of freight transport expected to show significant gains through to 2020 are maritime transport and long-haul trucking.

To an important extent, the remarkable increase in international transportation witnessed in recent decades is linked to the growing phenomenon of the internationalisation of production systems. The various

THE SECURITY ECONOMY – ISBN 92-64-10772-X – © OECD 2004

component stages of economic activity – R&D, technological development, production, distribution, marketing, etc. – have increasingly become organised into global value chains that have themselves become more fragmented as business functions are differentiated into ever more specialised activities. More recently, supply chains have extended into new areas of the globe, integrating formerly distinct regional production activities. In addition there is a growing tendency for firms, even large multinational enterprises, to specialise more narrowly and to contract out more and more functions to independent firms, spreading them internationally to exploit differences in costs and logistics. The upshot is the creation of worldwide supply chains that are increasingly widely dispersed, highly complex, and very vulnerable to disruption, delay and criminal operations.

By way of illustration, and using the example of two economies that share a common border, it is estimated that disruptions to the US-Canadian border through terrorist activity could affect up to 45% of all of Canada's exports, about 400 000 jobs and USD 2.5 billion in investments.

Most indications suggest that many of the forces that created these highly dispersed global value chains are likely to persist well into the future. Pressure to drive down supply chain costs from product design to delivery seems unrelenting, so that firms continue to be forced to relocate or outsource segments of their supply chain.

Moreover, the pursuit of new foreign markets will often lead to supply lines being stretched further as trade restrictions come into play and the price for market access may be local production or local sourcing. Finally, making

Figure 8. **The global supply line cost squeeze**

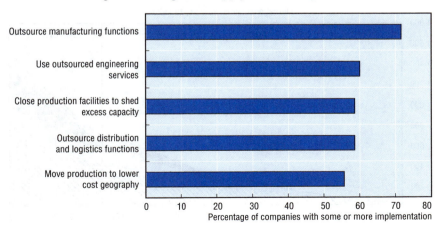

Source: Deloitte, Touche LLP, 2003a.

inroads into new foreign markets means requiring supply chains to effectively deliver products that suit local tastes – on time, in the right quantity and quality, and at the right cost. As the speed of innovation picks up and product life cycles become shorter, the demands on supply chains are magnified. Hence, securing global supply networks is set to become a major corporate challenge in the coming years.

4. Operational efficiency

Quite aside from the issue of security, increasing competition and rising expectations of consumers, citizens and businesses all add impetus to the drive for greater efficiency in operations and procedures. As controls at ports and airports tighten, for example, they can lead to disruptive and damaging delays in the supply of essential products, and moving masses of vehicles through toll facilities can lead to major congestion. Transiting hundreds of thousands of air passengers through ever stricter passport and customs controls costs time and can result in large productivity losses. Tourism offers an instructive view of the future in this respect. Figure 9 indicates that international tourist arrivals worldwide are anticipated to triple over the 25 years between 1995 and 2020 to about 1.6 billion, with the proportion of long-haul trips growing much more quickly than that within regions.

As the above section has shown, mobility is on the rise and the coming years are likely to witness further significant increases in flows of people and

Figure 9. **Projections of international tourist arrivals to 2020**

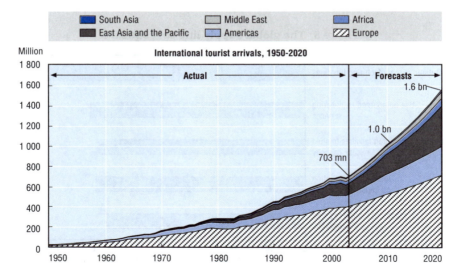

Source: World Tourism Organization, Tourism Highlights 2003.

goods through public facilities, across frontiers and so on. Thus, the search for quick, efficient, cost-effective solutions to problems of this nature promises to be an important driver behind the emergence of ever more innovative and sophisticated identification and surveillance technologies.

5. The growing need for information security

One of the most significant changes over the past few decades has been the rise of information as a strategically important, integral part of everyday economic and social life. This growing importance of information has been compounded by the increasing use of electronic commerce. As a consequence, millions of firms face very costly threats from theft of information (intellectual property, customer data, etc.), financial fraud, or quite simply disruption of their information systems through targeted security breaches or more generalised viruses or worms. Regular surveys (e.g. CSI/FBI, PWC/DTI, Deloitte, etc.) show that in the last couple of years between two-fifths and three-fifths of firms have experienced serious information security breaches, often resulting in considerable financial losses.

While the frequency of attacks from internal sources remains significant, those stemming from the Internet are clearly on the rise. According to global surveys – for example the Symantec Internet Threat Report – among the organisations most frequently targeted are power and energy companies and financial services firms. However, the evidence indicates that the risk of cyber attacks and malicious code infections remains high for all Internet-connected organisations.

A number of factors are likely to contribute to continuing vulnerability over the next few years, among them:

- The introduction of entirely new and potentially more destructive forms of malicious code and cyber attacks.
- The proliferation of new web applications, many of which have relatively straightforward remote accessibility that is easy to exploit.
- The spread of (often unauthorised) use of instant messaging applications and peer-to-peer applications.
- The growth of mobile devices with always-on connectivity and remote access to critical sensitive data.

Interestingly, the expansion of ICT infrastructure also appears to be adding to information system vulnerability. Korea, for example, has put a major effort into the development of consumer broadband infrastructure in recent years, with considerable success. But as broadband becomes more accessible, it also becomes more exposed to malicious activity. Thus Korea also currently figures among the countries with the highest occurrence of attacks per 10 000 Internet users. Several eastern European countries with rapidly growing Internet user rates also rank high on the list of "attacking" countries.

Hence, as the vulnerability of information systems persists and evolves, demand for information security – both for physical security and access control (*e.g.* biometrics, encryption login) and for operational security (firewalls, anti-virus software, etc.) – is expected to grow.

6. Institutional and organisational change

With the growing appreciation of threats to security, institutional and organisational reforms have been set in train which are having – and will continue to have – a significant impact on the level and structure of demand for security goods and services. Governments across the world have been reviewing their national ID systems – from issuance procedures to verification of documents' authenticity through law enforcement bodies or through customs. As a result, many public installations and organisations have begun to tighten their ID security. Governments have been looking to upgrade not only passports but also other secure documents such as visas, voter registration cards, driving licences, and of course ID cards.

In some cases, reviews have led to wholesale restructuring of the institutional architecture. Perhaps the most striking recent example of this kind of development is the creation of the US Department for Homeland Security (DHS) in the aftermath of the terrorist attacks of September 11. The Department was created by merging 22 different agencies and programmes into a cabinet-level department with four major directorates: Border and Transportation Security, Emergency Preparedness and Response, Science and Technology, and Information Analysis and Infrastructure Protection. The creation of DHS incorporated half of the government's homeland security funding (currently around USD 38 billion) within a single agency. The DHS budget rose by two-thirds between financial years 2002 and 2003, from over USD 11 billion to USD 19 billion. Figure 10 below shows the implications of the creation of DHS for homeland-security related funding across relevant departments.

Such restructuring, with its budgetary consequences, is not restricted to the United States. In Germany, for example, a new "strategy for the protection of the population in Germany" has been agreed which entails a bundling of the federal government's responsibilities for managing natural catastrophes, industrial accidents, infectious diseases and international terrorism, as well as the creation of a new federal agency for civil protection and disaster. In a similar vein, Norway has just established an agency for emergency management and civil protection; its budget is expected to rise by over 60% between 2003 and 2004.

Broader changes in national legislation are also likely to have important implications for spending on security goods and services. By way of

Figure 10. **US Government spending on Homeland Security**

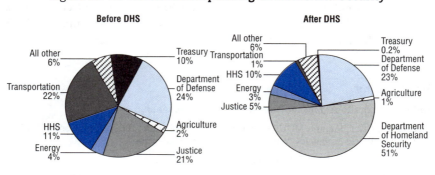

Source: Report to Congress on Combating Terrorism, 2003.

illustration, Italy is in the process of introducing nationwide a new high-security ID card which will be phased in over a period of five years (see Chapter 5 of this volume); and the United Kingdom's Home Secretary announced plans in the Autumn of 2003 to introduce compulsory ID cards that will be based on biometric characteristics of the cardholder. Moreover, a number of new governance initiatives are emerging worldwide that can be expected to have a considerable impact on the management of security in government agencies and corporations. In the financial field, for instance, initiatives such as the Basel Accord and the Personal Information Protection and Electronic Documents Act (PIPEDA) are putting more emphasis on the introduction of more controls and on holding management accountable for the integrity and representation of their financial information.

Finally, the corporate sector itself is undergoing significant changes in the wake of tightening security. In the United States, major private sector companies are expected to spend between USD 46 billion and USD 76 billion in fiscal year 2003 on Homeland Security-related activities. Some of the larger corporations have already established their own homeland security departments to lend better focus to the security effort. Specifically on the information security front, worldwide surveys point to some important organisational changes under way in multinational companies. Since the mid-1990s especially, the more forward-looking firms have begun to raise the reporting level of their information security functions significantly so as to give them more authority and access. Today, a large number of these corporations have a Chief Security Officer or a Chief Information Security Officer.

These, then, are the economic, social and institutional factors that are set to shape the demand for security in the coming years. How the prospects actually unfold will of course also depend on other factors – not least technological change in the security sector's offerings, how quickly new and more sophisticated technologies become affordable, and of course how acceptable such technologies will prove to be to the general public. These issues are the subject of discussion in the chapters that follow.

Bibliography

AIRBUS (2002), Global Market Forecast 2001-2020, Blagnac.

ATKINSON, Giles, Susana MOURATO and Andrew HEALEY (2003), "The Cost of Violent Crime", World Economics, Vol. 4, No. 4, October-December.

BOEING (2002), World Air Cargo Forecast 2002/2003, Seattle.

BUNDESMINISTERIUM DER FINANZEN (2002), Finanzplan des Bundes 2002-2006, Berlin.

BUNDESMINISTERIUM DER FINANZEN (2003), Finanzplan des Bundes 2003-2007, Berlin.

BUNDESVERBAND DEUTSCHER WACH- UND SICHERHEITSUNTERNEHMEN, Miscellaneous statistics.

CANADIAN DEPARTMENT OF FINANCE (2001), The Budget in Brief 2001, Ottawa.

CANADIAN DEPARTMENT OF FINANCE (2003), The Budget in Brief 2003, Ottawa.

COMPUTER SECURITY INSTITUTE/FEDERAL BUREAU OF INVESTIGATION (2003), Computer Crime and Security Survey, San Francisco.

CONFEDERATION OF EUROPEAN SECURITY SERVICES (2003), Annual Report 2003, Wemmel, 20 October.

COUNCIL OF EUROPE (2002), Organised Crime Situation Report 2001, Strasbourg.

DELOITTE, TOUCHE and TOHMATSU (2003), 2003 Global Security Survey, New York, May.

DELOITTE, TOUCHE LLP (2003a), The Challenge of Complexity in Global Manufacturing: Critical Trends in Supply Chain Management, London.

DELOITTE, TOUCHE LLP (2003b), Mastering Complexity in Global Manufacturing: Powering Profit and Growth through Value Chain Synchronization, London.

The Economist (2003), "Crime in Japan", 25 October.

EUROPOL (2002), 2000 European Union Organised Crime Situation, The Hague.

EXECUTIVE OFFICE OF THE PRESIDENT OF THE UNITED STATES (2002), Budget for Fiscal Year 2003, Washington DC.

EXECUTIVE OFFICE OF THE PRESIDENT OF THE UNITED STATES (2003a), Budget for Fiscal Year 2004, Washington DC.

EXECUTIVE OFFICE OF THE PRESIDENT OF THE UNITED STATES (2003b), Report to Congress on Combating Terrorism, Washington DC.

FEDERAL BUREAU OF INVESTIGATION (2002), Crime in the United States – 2002, Washington DC.

INTERNATIONAL ORGANIZATION FOR MIGRATION (2003), "Facts and Figures on International Migration", Migration Policy, No. 2, March.

INTERPOL (2003), Crime statistics of selected countries, 1995 and 2002.

J.P. FREEMAN REPORTS (2003), US and Worldwide CCTV and Digital Video Surveillance Market Report, J.P. Freeman et al., Newtown, CT.

LAMBLIN, Véronique (2003), "Le développement des résidences sécurisées", Futuribles, No. 291, November.

LLOYD, Carolyn (2003), "Is Secure Trade Replacing Free Trade?" in John M. Curtis and Dan Ciurak (eds.), Trade Policy Research, Minister of Public Works and Government Services, Canada.

OECD (2001), OECD Environmental Outlook, OECD, Paris.

OECD (2002), Trends in International Migration 2001, OECD, Paris.

OECD (2003), Emerging Systemic Risks in the 21st Century, OECD, Paris.

POPULATION REFERENCE BUREAU (2002), "International Migration: Facing the Challenge", Population Bulletin, 57:1, March.

PRICEWATERHOUSECOOPERS (2002), Information Security Breaches Survey 2002: Technical Report, Department of Trade and Industry, London.

RANSTORP, M. (2003), Statement to the National Commission on Terrorist Attacks Upon the United States, 31 March.

RUTTENBUR, Brian (2002), "Biometrics and Security Update", NextInnovator, 25 November, http:technologyreports.net.

SECURITY INDUSTRY ASSOCIATION, Miscellaneous industry statistics.

Smart Labels Analyst (2003), "RFID in Asia", Issue 32, September.

SYMANTEC (2003), "Internet Security Threat Report", Symantec, Cupertino, CA, February.

SYNDICAT NATIONAL DES ENTERPRISES DE SÉCURITÉ, Miscellaneous statistics.

UK HOME OFFICE (2001), British Crime Survey 2001, London.

UK NATIONAL CRIMINAL INTELLIGENCE SERVICE (2003), United Kingdom Threat Assessment of Serious and Organised Crime 2003, London.

UN POPULATION (2002), International Migration Report 2002, New York.

UN POPULATION (2003), World Population Prospects: The 2002 Revision: Highlights, New York, February.

UNCTAD (2002), World Investment Report 2002: Transnational Corporations and Export Competitiveness: Overview, Geneva.

US CONFERENCE OF MAYORS (2003), First Mayors' Report to the Nation: Tracking Federal Homeland Security Funds – Sent to the 50 State Governments, September.

US DEPARTMENT OF TRANSPORT (2000), Criminal Acts Against Aviation Report, Washington DC.

WILKINSON, Paul (2003), "Observations on the New Terrorism", Statement to the UK Foreign Affairs Committee, June.

WORLD BANK (2003), Global Economic Prospects 2004, Washington DC.

WORLD TOURISM ORGANIZATION (2003), Tourism Highlights 2003, Madrid.

ISBN 92-64-10772-X
The Security Economy
OECD 2004

Chapter 3

Biometrics

by

Bernard Didier
Technical and Business Development
SAGEM SA
France

1. A short introduction to Biometrics

"Open Sesame"

All the magic of recognition – and all the foibles – are wrapped up in this little phrase from an oriental fable. Recognising, identifying and authenticating are needs that go back to the dawn of time.

The ancient Chinese authenticated property deeds with fingerprints. Egyptian potters knew that the prints they left in the clay would identify their wares. Epistemology is fond of rediscovered inventions: it was not until the second half of the 19th century that biometric methods cropped up again, in the work of William Herschel, who came upon the idea, in Bengal in 1858, of sealing contractual documents with palm prints. Thus was born the best known, and undoubtedly the most widespread and proven, technique of identification: the fingerprint. This was followed sometime later, in 1883, by Alphonse Bertillon, who introduced anthropometric techniques for identifying habitual criminals. In that same year, the fingerprint identification technique made its way into a novel, *Life on the Mississippi*, written by one Samuel Clemens, better known by his pen name, Mark Twain.

With the conquest of the West and the spread of the telegraph, telegraph operators soon developed a characteristic code that allowed them to be recognised. This technique was commonly used during the Second World War to authenticate senders and receivers. It was in the middle of the 1960s, when the identification of repeat offenders from their fingerprints had been recognised and used for decades by police all over the world, that the FBI finally launched an ambitious research programme on the automatic processing of fingerprints. It was at this same time that Stanford University demonstrated it was possible to "discriminate" a population of some 5 000 individuals by measuring the length of the fingers of one hand. This biometric technique was used experimentally to control entry into examination halls. It gave rise to the first system of biometric access control, known by the name "Identimat". That breakthrough opened up several paths of research for improving a technique that was still in its infancy.

Some definitions and consequences

The fundamental purpose of biometric procedures is to "identify" or "authenticate" individuals.

Identification

"Identification" should be understood as any approach for describing each person within a known population in a unique manner so that it is always possible to demonstrate whether a given person is, or is not, a member of that known population. This definition calls for several comments:

- Finding a unique and immutable description of each person is the fundamental principle governing the construction of a biometric technique.

- The difficulty of achieving a unique description will grow with the size of the population in question (which may surpass that of the known population).[1] It is easy to manage the identity of a dozen people, using certain elementary physical criteria (hair or eye colour, sex, size, etc.), but these criteria are clearly inadequate for managing the population of a country. Intuitively, one can see that a description that is too superficial will produce homonyms (mistaken identifications) while a description that is too detailed, if it does not adhere strictly to the principle of immutability, runs the risk of non-identification (persons mistakenly identified).

- Identification is a process that involves comparing the unique description of an individual against all the known descriptions of the population, and then deciding which is the identical one. This comparison of one individual to all other individuals is known as a "one to n" comparison (written as "1:n").

Authentication

Authentication is understood as any approach whereby a trusted third party or certification authority can describe an individual in such a way that it is subsequently possible to verify whether a person fits the authentic description. Some comments:

- The notion of "trusted third party", while not very explicit, is of great importance in the act of authentication. The quality of authentication depends on this trusted third party.[2]

- The authentication description can be memorised either in a file, in which case the person to be authenticated must provide the information needed to find that description and so proceed to verification, or in a medium (a smartcard, for example, or a passport) held by the person to be authenticated. In the latter case, authentication, unlike identification, does not necessarily imply constructing a file of personal descriptions.

- Authentication does not implicate the individual's identity: the description fits or it does not. Nevertheless, the quality of any authentication depends on the prior existence of an identification function: in effect, providing the same person with several means of authentication, under different identifications, introduces a security weak spot.

● Authentication consists of verifying whether a person's description is identical to the authentic or prior description associated with that person. This operation of comparing one description to another is called "one to one" comparison (written "1:1").

Identifying and authenticating: two complementary approaches

Generally speaking, system security depends on the carefully combined use of these two functions. During the granting of a right, identification serves to verify that the petitioner is not subject to a prohibition and that they do not already exist in the system under another name. It is at this stage also that the biometric reference information (template) is created, which will later serve to authenticate the applicant when they attempt to exercise their right.

All biometric techniques offer authenticating functions, but they do not necessarily allow for identification. Only those techniques that are fundamentally based on person-specific biometric information can correctly fulfil this function. Historically, fingerprinting was the first technique to allow both identification and authentication. In the current state of the art, apart from the iris and DNA, there are no really effective authentication techniques.

His master's voice… or finger, or eye

What are the physical criteria that can be used to authenticate a person? On this point imagination runs wild, and each successive fashion of the moment sends shudders through the tight little world of biometrics, which fears that novelty will win out over quality. The accepted physical criteria fall into two broad categories: knowledge approaches and anatomical approaches.

Knowledge approaches authenticate individuals through their capacity to reproduce, repeatedly and consistently, certain muscular movements. This category includes dynamic signature analysis, voice recognition, keystroke analysis. But these techniques are vulnerable over time.

Anatomical techniques are based on processing certain physical features that are considered immutable and unique to each individual. The most common characteristics in this class are fingerprints, DNA, the iris, ear shape, and the vein geometry of the hand. This category also includes face recognition. These features, in particular the first ones, are intrinsically stable over time, and any changes detected are often due to artefacts in the information acquisition system.

Assessing the performance of biometric systems

Preliminary remark

Any performance evaluation should be approached as a systemic analysis that looks at the performance of the overall security function. In this regard, we can distinguish security performances that are extrinsic to the choice of biometric technology (physical security element; physical difficulty of breaking the system and its logic; use of cryptography techniques) from those that are intrinsic to that choice, such as the error rate or the capacity to reproduce the biometric element artificially. This comprehensive approach, which is still known as "protection profile policy", and on which the French Government's position is rather unclear, deserves special attention. Initially, analysis will be reduced to measuring errors.

Failure to Enrol (FTE)

FTE is the percentage of the population unable to register. All biometric systems have trouble with certain population classes. For example, there are problems in fingerprinting with manual labourers; in iris recognition with people whose irises are very pale (such as Nordic persons) or very dark (such as certain Africans); the faces of certain ethnic groups are hard to process (the Australian border control pilot system mistook Japanese faces at an official demonstration run). The percentage varies depending on the strategy – it may be decided to register at all costs, but this will simply shift the problem to the identification or authentication stage.[3] Even the best system suppliers will have an FTE rate of 1 to 2% for fingerprints and irises.

False Match Rate (FMR)

The FMR is the percentage of individuals wrongly declared identical during an identification or authentication procedure. The consequences depend on the use. For access control, an unauthorised person will have been wrongly granted access (false acceptance). In a "watch list" type of operation, the result will be false identification with an individual who is to be excluded (false rejection). In a multiple enrolment detection operation, the applicant will be wrongly rejected. It is important to understand that these two rates (false acceptance and false rejection) are correlated: if the system is set to detect all impostors, then many more people will be mistakenly blocked.[4]

False Non-Match Rate (FNMR)

The FNMR is the percentage of individuals who are wrongly declared different. Again, the consequences of such errors will be clear in light of use.

The accuracy of different biometric techniques

For any single technology, performance may vary significantly from one supplier to the next in terms of authentication. The average performance of different independent industry sources is summarised in the following table:

Table 1. **Technology performance**

	Face	Fingerprint	Iris
FTE	0 – 5%	0 – 1%	0 – 3%
FMR (FAR)	1.0%	0.1%	> 0%
FNMR (FRR)	10 – 40%	0.5 – 1%	2 – 3%

Sources: US Department of Defense; Defense Advanced Research Projects Agency; National Institute of Justice; Communications-Electronics Security Group (UK); Bologna University; US National Biometric Test Center; Israeli Basel Project; and different benchmarks.

These average values shed some light on choices for small-scale access control operations, for example, but it would be very risky to extrapolate these values and draw conclusions from them when considering systems that affect state security and need to cover tens of millions of people. In this case, even low error rates would imply a manual validation burden that would be prohibitive.

2. Segmentation: the different uses of biometrics

Segmentation is difficult

The biometrics industry is not monolithic; proper segmentation of markets, products and players is a precondition for any analysis of this industry. Some biometric market studies have suffered in the past from a failure to define these segments clearly, and have led to some rather surprising business forecasts.

The market is certainly hard to assess, because there is very little public information about it and there are a great many players. More importantly, as markets have evolved, the chain of value in this sector has become more complex. In the early 1980s, there were only two major classes of players: those who manufactured the biometric access control packages, using a fairly primitive access control system, and those who made fingerprinting systems for police work. The 1990s saw repeated swings between "horizontalisation" and "verticalisation" of players in the industry:

- Some players attempted to focus solely on the biometric sensors subsegment, fingerprint readers in particular.
- One group was more particularly interested in live-scan police booking stations, at a time when police forces were moving away from "inking"

techniques and towards the "paperless" office. Some of these players refined their products towards acquisition subsystems or towards background check functions. Given the quality demands, there are few players in this sector, despite the sharp growth occasioned by September 11, 2001.

- A second class of players emerged from the electronic components industry (primarily Infinion, ST Microelectronics, Atmel) to offer low-cost sensors for securing laptop computers, PDAs and cell phones. The slow growth of those markets, however, has led these players either to withdraw or to verticalise on logical or physical access control solutions, while waiting for better days.

- Middleware companies appeared: either "pure" technology firms such as East Shore Technology, or multimodal biometric solution firms such as I/O Software and Keyware. Consistent with the middleware trend, biometric packages have evolved towards interfaces compatible with industrial access control or time management systems, and away from proprietary solutions. Similarly, solutions are becoming more and more integrated (Daon or Activcard, for example) with generic off-the-shelf products [document management, ERP (Enterprise Resource Planning), PKI (Public Key Infrastructure)].

- Large-scale integrators appeared, offering complex systems or management services for institutional passes, in which biometrics becomes a commodity, like chip cards.

This complexity in the value chain makes it particularly difficult to analyse the biometrics market's evolution from an economic viewpoint, in terms of direct and indirect revenues. It will take a permanent effort on the part of the various biometrics industry associations to make the business financially more transparent. Given the current scepticism about new technologies, such transparency is a prerequisite if this newly emerging sector of activity is to develop and win credibility in the eyes of financial players and potential clients.

Using biometrics to combat crime: the police market

These police systems are usually grouped under the acronym AFIS (Automatic Fingerprint Identification Systems). They can identify individuals from imprints of their ten fingers, but they differ from other institutional or civil systems in their capacity to identify indistinct or partial fingerprint traces left at the scene of the crime.

It took a full decade for these systems – the fruits of research undertaken first at the behest of the FBI back in the 1970s, primarily by Calspan Autonetics and Rockwell – to gain the confidence of the American police community. Originally, the automatic identification techniques used by the police made little use of biometrics, which were mainly limited to access control in the civilian sphere. It was not until the end of the last century, with the increasing use of AFIS systems for management of civil identity passes, that the use of biometrics was extended to large-scale identification systems. Today, nearly all modern police forces are so equipped.

In technical terms, these systems can handle thousands of identifications a day from a database covering millions or even tens of millions of individuals. The latest system acquired by the FBI, in the mid-1990s, performs some 40 000 searches a day from a population of 40 million, and is the most powerful in the world.

In industrial terms, the systems are provided by companies that market, install and develop AFIS. There are three historic players – NEC (Japan), Printrack, which was recently acquired by Motorola (United States), and SAGEM (France) – and a relative newcomer, Cogent (United States). SAGEM is the current world leader[5] in this market segment, as demonstrated by both its sales volume[6] and its prestigious clients, in particular the FBI and Interpol.

In economic terms, these systems have probably accounted for the most significant ongoing investments that police forces have made over the last 20 years in the information processing field (apart from telecommunications). Thanks to the installation of such systems, the crime solution rate has jumped fivefold to tenfold, with an apparent, if not yet quantified, impact on property values. This is a mature segment of the market, limited essentially to replacement purchases, amounting to some USD 150 million to USD 200 million a year.

The segment also includes the makers of biometric live-scan booking stations for police use. This equipment may be sold as part of the systems described above, or in separate orders. These companies' revenues amounted to USD 100 million in 2001, shared between the leader Identix (following its merger with Visionics DBII), CrossMatch and Heimann Biometric Systems.

Institutional biometric systems

This market segment is involved in managing the delivery and use of institutional proof of rights or eligibility such as ID cards, pensions, social security, passports and visas. Demand on this market is relatively recent, dating from 1992/93. There is a dual objective here: to ensure that the same right is not accorded to the same person more than once or to an unauthorised person, and to control the authenticity of the person seeking to exercise a right. For the most part, automatic fingerprint processing systems are used.

On the technical level, AFIS is only one of the elements of a more complex solution, based on the manufacture of secure ID cards that allow for the subsequent verification of the holder by fingerprint analysis, and that may include civil status particulars. These systems apply to bigger populations than crime-fighting systems, and have to meet very heavy performance demands involving the identification of tens of thousands of individuals from databases of many millions of people. The sheer size of the flows involved requires different and more complex structures than the AFIS used for police purposes. Systematic, massive authentication takes precedence over subtle trace identification.

In industry practice, responses to government tenders are channelled through consortia led by "integrators" (TRW, Unisys, Siemens, IBM, etc.) and including the traditional AFIS manufacturers (Motorola, NEC, SAGEM, and Cogent) and the card manufacturers (Polaroid, Gemplus, Oberthur, Gesiecke and Devrient, etc.). In this market, SAGEM has reaped the majority of contracts, either as the AFIS manufacturer or, as in some recent cases, by offering a complete service as "integrator", manufacturing the AFIS and producing the secure cards.

It is a developing market segment of approximately USD 50-100 million a year, with long decision cycles (more than three years). It can be estimated that total contracts signed over the last ten years have covered perhaps 275 million people.[7] It is primarily in Asia, the Middle East and Africa that large-scale civil status or identity card projects are being pursued. Europe has used this approach essentially for managing asylum-seekers (EURODAC), while the United States has applied it to the delivery of social benefits. Since the events of September 11, this market segment has been hit by a good deal of turbulence, with the announcement that biometric passports and visas are imminent, and with the (still uncertain) move to biometric ID cards (Georgia and Oklahoma in the United States, the "Entitlement Card" in the United Kingdom, the titre fondateur in France). As a result, an institutional market is rapidly emerging for fingerprint booking station – once the preserve of the police – and prices for this equipment can be expected to fall sharply.

With the recently growing insistence on prior identity checks of applicants for jobs in certain sensitive fields (airports, transportation of funds, etc.), some American states have been encouraging the supply of such services.

It is a market segment that has its own built-in dynamics: a state that provides itself with a biometrically secured smartcard is likely to encourage its use for other purposes than simply controlling entitlement use. Malaysia, for example, has launched the GMPC (Government Multi-Purpose Card), a fingerprint-secured ID card that incorporates driving licence, passport and e-cash functions, and the United Arab Emirates is introducing a multi-application ID card.

Biometric systems for commercial and industrial use

After appearing as prototypes in the mid-1970s, the first commercial products were put on the market in the early 1980s. They were originally targeted at access control and time management uses, their clients being governmental entities (prisons, for example) and, more rarely, commercial and industrial companies. In the latter case, "back end" applications prevailed over "front end" uses. For two or three years now, biometric security solutions for commercial transactions have been appearing in the United States, with Biopay (check cashing), BAC and Indivos.

In technical terms, the most widely used technologies were, historically, fingerprinting and finger-length measurement. These have recently been joined by facial recognition and iris scanning. Solutions proposed may range from a biometric captor (most frequently a fingerprint scanner) connected to a PC with processing software, to an access control box, fulfilling authentication and perhaps identification functions. In the latter case, thousands of fingerprints are compared.

At the industrial level, sales are often made by "integrators", distributors, or companies specialised in vertical market segments (transport, health, etc.). The equipment is designed by a myriad (more than 140 in early 2001) of small firms of varying solidity, that only rarely have the capacity for production and performance evaluation of their technology. The years 1998-2001 saw the beginnings of consolidation,[8] marked in particular by the takeover of Identicator by Identix for USD 43 million, and the problems of Veridicom (a company that nevertheless boasted some significant shareholders, such as Intel, ATT and Lucent Technologies) and Ethentica (with shareholders such as Citibank and Philips Electronics). The latter owed its survival to the injection of USD 40 million and the enlistment of HP and Amdhal as investors. Consolidation should continue, leaving perhaps a dozen firms, as no "lone player" in this market segment is making money.

The historic players here are Identix, ST Microelectonics for fingerprint processing, Iridian for iris scanning, Cognitec, Visionics and Viisage for face recognition. Two years ago SAGEM came in, offering police-tested technologies that are not readily available to traditional companies in this market segment, and promptly landed some high-profile clients (the *Postes d'inspection filtrages des Aéroports de Paris* screening services, for one). In 2003, SAGEM expanded its offerings with original iris and face recognition solutions developed in strategic partnership with Iridian and Cognitec.

Despite its age, this is a still budding market segment, but it is developing rapidly. The traditional access control and time management subsegment has recently been joined by demand for logical access control (PC, Internet and

Intranet transactions, etc.), which will likely be followed by demand for personal equipment (PDA and telephone).

The market for biometrics terminals is the object of somewhat diverging market analyses. Depending on the source,[9, 10, 11, 12] it was valued at between USD 66 and USD 196 million in 2000, all technologies included. Accepting that, as is the case for access control systems (but not for the PC and PDA markets), biometric scanners represent perhaps 10% of system sales, they are probably generating indirect revenues of more than USD 1 billion.

On the other hand, a consensus holds that fingerprint analysis is the market's favoured technique. A majority of analysts estimate that, with a market share of between 37% and 55% and a growth rate of at least 40% per annum, fingerprinting is the most promising technology among biometrics products.

Biometric systems for personal use

This segment is still in its infancy. The year 2003 has seen confirmation of fingerprint-secured laptop computers (from Samsung in particular), the significant emergence in Japan of the first cell phones with fingerprint sensors (Fujitsu), and the first PDAs (HP Compact).

The watchword for this market is comfort rather than security. It remains the privileged domain of the scanner manufacturers (ST Microelectronics, Infineon, Atmel), and is essentially a component sales market.

Conclusion

In practical terms, automatic fingerprint recognition systems are most often used today in various applications. Fingerprint biometrics represents more than 50% of the biometric techniques used around the world. This finding merely underscores a known fact: the maturity of fingerprint technology is based on more than a century of usage and on nearly half a century of industrial investments, sparked by demand from governments eager to support their police forces in fighting crime.

3. Tomorrow's markets

The last century, the coming century...

The past century saw the emergence of biometric techniques. Fingerprinting dominated the century with worldwide use, and generated the first industrial forays into automatic biometric data processing. The end of the century saw the birth of a stronger biometric movement, with the beginnings of face, voice, iris and even ear recognition, and most importantly, DNA tracing. It is safe to predict that the coming century will bring all these new techniques to maturity, for purposes of either comfort or security.

In economic life, the state-citizen relationship and most organisational activities rely essentially on a visible or implicit bond of trust. Historically, officials responsible for national defence and security developed a body of techniques for validating the authenticity of information and orders so as to carry out their missions more effectively. "The Romans' secret code" offered a guarantee of secrecy and authenticity while, closer to our times, the wax seal merely represented an effort, today discarded, to confirm the authenticity of the document.

The last hundred years represented the "cryptological" century. From Turing to public key infrastructure, there is a visible continuity of efforts and issues. States today rely on these techniques to guarantee the security of their transmissions and the authenticity of messages. Yet it is no longer reasonable to be satisfied with this approach alone: the next hundred years will be the "biometric century".

The key to the confidentiality function lies in the possession of an object (increasingly a smartcard) and the knowledge of the secret. Traditional approaches, based on the possession of an object (IT) or secret (a password), offered no guarantee of the formal identity of the possessor of the object or the secret. The rise of identity theft, particularly in the United States, and the growing instances of ATM fraud are sufficient examples. For once, politicians have been in the vanguard in their awareness of the missing link between the living world and the material/virtual world.

As with any new technology, and now perhaps more than formerly, the use of biometrics will entail much debate in society about the threats it poses – to individual liberty among other things. The ultimate balance will depend on the choices that society makes, but also on society's capacity to understand that these techniques, which may represent an attack on individual liberties, can also be just as effective at defending personal data, assets, identity – in other words, property. Biometrics will then be assessed by the yardstick of the systemic risk of collapse of the virtual economic world.

After September 11

Some of the denizens of the small world of biometrics, followed indeed by the stock exchanges, tended to think, in the aftermath of September 11, that the demand for biometrics would explode. In fact, while shares of these companies may have tripled by their peak in December, they sank back to their pre-9/11 value in September 2002, as their operating statements reflected the jump in marketing costs with little offsetting additional revenue.

THE SECURITY ECONOMY – ISBN 92-64-10772-X – © OECD 2004

In fact, governments first stepped up investment in the products they were already using: bomb detectors, crisis management centres and command stations. The use of new technological approaches, such as biometrics, appeared only later, and in a manner integrated into complex structures: visa and passport management systems. This integrated approach, which turns biometrics into a commodity, is the price that has to be paid for recognition and the beginnings of maturity in the field. Institutional applications based on reciprocity of treatment will accelerate the emergence of standards and the generalised use of these techniques. More and more citizens will hold smartcards, thus sowing the seeds for a more widespread use of biometrics in the future.

The breakdown of the "business model"

The past has shown that biometrics developed significantly in government applications, but lagged behind in commercial and industrial applications. That pattern probably reflects political rather than economic choices. The political impact of introducing biometric ID cards or passports, or crime control systems, is undeniable, whereas the economic return, while it is there, is hard to discern. The economy will move on, or rather it will dig in its heels against the use of biometrics, as soon as the targeted market raises privacy concerns: this is what happened in the market for social benefits in the United States, which regularly worries about the return on investment. The level of detected cases of fraud, which is very low but known, outweighs the dissuasive effect of biometrics, which is economically very significant but has never been the object of serious study.

On commercial markets, and particularly for financial transactions, despite the sharp drop in prices for the technology (which in the case of fingerprint solutions declined by a factor of 10 over the last five years), no one is anticipating much of a return from fraud prevention. Users do not see why they should pay for a debit card security device when the issuing bank guarantees them against any loss from fraud; the banks, for their part, will either have recourse to the merchants or charge a provision for risk on client accounts; and merchants will build a risk factor into their price. There is in effect a "non-virtuous" circle that makes it very difficult to sell biometric security equipment. Only a major systemic risk[13, 14] or a worldwide player bent on sharp differentiation could break this circle and demonstrate clear economic value.

The rising trend in identity theft

Faced with a wave of identity theft in the United States, the Federal Trade Commission (FTC) has set up an organisation to track this type of crime. Its latest survey, dated 3 September 2003, was accompanied by an alarming press release showing that:

Over the last five years,

- 27.3 million American citizens or residents were victims of identity theft.
- Losses to businesses and financial institutions amounted to USD $48 billion.
- Consumer victims were out of pocket USD 5 billion.

In the last year alone,

- 9.9 million US citizens or residents were victims of ID theft.
- 3.23 million consumers found that new accounts had been opened in their name.
- 1.5 million people reported that their personal information was misused in nonfinancial ways, such as to obtain government documents, or on tax forms.
- 5 million people discovered that they were victims by monitoring their accounts.
- 2.5 million victims were alerted by their bank.
- 800 000 people discovered the incident after their account was drawn down.

This very worrying situation is clearly grounds for rethinking the security of payments and the mechanisms for delivering identity instruments or government documents. The move to the new smartcard standard (EMV) in Europe should go some way towards a solution, but at the same time it will heighten the interest of fraud artists in finding ways to attack secret codes. Extending this approach to all of a user's cards also poses a not inconsiderable problem for facility of use. In this context, biometrics could play a significant role, provided some of the current difficulties are resolved.

Market trends

The crime-fighting market

This market is unlikely to see the kind of upheavals experienced during the last century. Fingerprint systems based on fully computerised solutions should make their way into the smallest police organisations and permit local or nationwide identification through network fixed or mobile microsystems.

The move to the paperless office and "background check" services using booking stations should accelerate over the next five years, as rising demand on institutional markets brings prices down.

After fingerprinting and DNA, the extension of biometric recognition to other features (the face for certain and probably the iris) would be a logical progression. Along with these technological choices, functions should evolve towards surveillance and, over the longer term, towards remote identification. Such fully biometric development will imply more sensitive and more complex issues for privacy protection agencies. This established market, which has grown to maturity on the basis of fingerprint systems, is likely to continue at a modest pace, as technology costs decline.

Institutional markets

These markets are likely to be dominated by international developments over the next five to ten years, with a focus on cross-border travel. The many players involved in each country, and the varying positions that countries take on the use of biometrics in light of privacy concerns, will likely mean the use of three basic biometric features: fingerprint, iris and face. The pressing need for interoperability, and the decisions that will be made in the next five years, will probably lead to some consolidation among market players.

On the domestic front, there will be some sharper differences in the choices that societies make about whether or not to introduce biometric identity. Given its history, Europe will probably be more inclined to countenance such instruments, probably with some built-in authentication functions. Even England, which has not been using these devices, could see some debate on the issue. The United States is likely to leave it to the states to decide on biometric driver's licences, and to abstain from imposing federal rules.

The real issue will revolve around the use of government-issued biometric ID cards: the state could provide everyone with a single ID card that allows for biometric authentication, and that can be used in dealings with all government agencies and services, obviating the need for (often ineffective) identification procedures. A special ID code for each service would protect people from unjustified sharing of personal information among agencies. This is the notion behind the *tire fondateur*[15] or electronic ID card, which in the end makes the government responsible for protecting the identity of citizens and residents.

Whatever choices governments make, border problems will encourage a more global approach: for example, people living in frontier zones who commute regularly across the border will be equipped with transit cards that are easier to use than a passport. This biometric card will likely come to be accorded the same legitimacy as an ID card.

Finally, identification services (background checks, for police or other purposes) should develop more quickly in countries that do not opt for ID cards, giving rise to multiple, fragmented and probably bigger markets.

All of these approaches will be subjected to evaluations and pilot projects, and it is likely that in some countries the armed forces (for whom security is necessarily a prime concern) will become the real incubators of biometrics use by government departments. This is already the case with the Common Access Card developed by the US Department of Defense.

This market should grow strongly over the next ten years.

Industrial and commercial markets

"Back end" markets will continue to grow, particularly in the area of physical access control, which will benefit from security requirements in transportation and at sensitive sites. The arrival of the first biometrically protected laptops should accelerate the spread of biometric access control solutions, particularly among users who travel frequently, and it should lead in time to generalised application of the biometric function in all information systems. The real issue in this market segment has to do with the breakdown of the existing "business model" and the use of biometrics in economic transactions. Some pioneer companies are building up a significant clientele. By early 2004, the Biopay programme will be used by more than one million Americans who have agreed voluntarily to have their fingerprints recorded.

Whether this market booms will depend on perceptions of the systemic risk of breakdown in the chain of confidentiality for financial transactions.[16] In the case of a breakdown, new models, based on a return per transaction, should generate even greater business than the institutional market. If there is no breakdown, the market should continue to grow steadily at a pace slightly faster than today's.

This market will benefit in any case from the low costs generated by the institutional market, and from the consolidation of players.

Personal use markets

This market is just emerging, with a focus on semiprofessional mobility products where convenience or comfort is more important than security (telephone, PDA, car). The lower costs that it implies should give rise to an inexpensive and mass-marketable biometric function: toys, safes, biometric locks. While it barely exists today, this market should begin to take shape within three to five years.

4. Challenges for the future

Technology

Technological research of a more or less exotic nature will continue, but technological issues will not be the main ones. In fact, the technologies that will supply the markets of tomorrow already exist. Instead, efforts will focus primarily on consolidating existing technologies, and on addressing such issues as these:

- Reinforcing scanners to support routine operating environments (primarily temperature, lighting and humidity).
- Developing non-participatory scanning techniques (surveillance by remote identification).
- Improving techniques for detecting biometric artefacts (false fingers, false iris, life-size facial photographs).
- Three-dimensional face imaging and development of tools for using existing photo archives.
- The definition of "sure" architecture based on "common criteria", such as those used with smartcards.
- Performance improvements, and in particular a drastic reduction in "Failure to Enrol" and "False Rejection Rate": this is essential in particular for the financial transactions market.
- Development of multi-biometric approaches that will improve performance and withstand impersonation attacks.

Respect for privacy

The traditional doctrines of privacy protection agencies, such as those relating to proportionality, purpose and traces,[17] will be challenged by the spreading use of biometrics and the many new techniques used by the police. Resolving these issues will require responsible communication and education on the part of all players: privacy protection agencies, governments, citizens and the industry. Solutions will be based on careful choices of legal and technical approaches.

In technical terms

The idea of identity does not rely strictly on biometric data. Identity is a set of attributes (civil status, address, photograph, personal data, ID number, etc.) that can be used to find an individual, for example. Biometric data alone, in the absence of attributes, can be used to ensure the proper delivery of a right, which can in itself be of interest without representing an attack on privacy. There are technical mechanisms for establishing a sure link between biometric data and attributes, with the prior approval of the individual concerned. There are also encryption methods that can be used under the control of a trusted third party.

Although there are mechanisms available that are practically irreversible, the precautionary principles adopted by privacy protection bodies insist that anything a manufacturer does can be undone by that same manufacturer, if the legal circumstances change.

In legal terms

Laws and regulations governing the use of biometric information for police investigation purposes can and should be developed to complement technical approaches. Every user can then appreciate, before beginning a transaction, how the biometric information they agree to provide might be used.

In terms of education, the identity-ownership duality needs to be given a new perspective: in any transaction, the aspect of "challenging a person's identity" often takes precedence over protecting that person's own assets.

The final question, from a legal point, is this: what responsibility does a government take upon itself by refusing to check the identity of passengers, for example, when it has the data and the means to identify terrorists?

Standards

When it comes to standards, the main question is the definition of interoperable biometric data formats that will keep pace with future technological advances. Today, given the limited resources of processing units and chip cards (in terms of memory, speed and power) to process data in a reasonable time, it would be well to anticipate authentication procedures by recording a reference template as the data format. This approach poses no essential problems for the automatic processing of fingerprints: the four worldwide players have a common description, i.e. the "characteristic points" of a fingerprint. This is not the case, however, when it comes to facial recognition, where the templates contain different and conflicting descriptions.

The record of information processing technologies leaves no doubt that within the next ten years it will be possible to store original biometric data as a compressed image. The standard will simply involve agreeing on the acquisition criteria and the compression technique to be used.

Meanwhile, there is nothing to prevent agreement on what is already feasible: using the future standard for fingerprint templates compiled from characteristic points ("minutiae"),[18] which should be stabilised by mid-2004.

Notes

1. For example, when it comes to institutional means of identification (ID cards, driver's licences), the objective is to distinguish and manage not only individuals who are known citizens of the state but to do the same with foreign residents or visitors. The population to be managed is distinct from and larger than the known population.

2. Take the example of a transaction at an automatic teller machine: the description that allows the person to be authenticated is "the person who knows the secret code yyyy". A person who enters this secret code is authenticated, but the validity of

this recognition, which implies handing over money, relies on the quality of the third party who defined and who manages the secret code. The concept of authentication of a right is therefore different from that of authentication of a person.

3. For example, the US Defense Department's Face Recognition Vendor Test (FRVT2002) set the FTE benchmark at zero.

4. Without going into technical details, this correlation between the two error rates will be intuitively apparent to any air traveller who has noted that, with recently heightened security precautions, metal detectors are producing more frequent false alarms.

5. The latest study by the American consulting firm Frost and Sullivan recognises SAGEM as the world leader, with a market share of 49.4% in terms of worldwide sales of AFIS systems in 2001.

6. Frost and Sullivan, *Global AFIS Market 2000*.

7. *Le marché mondial des Afis Civils*, SAGEM internal report, May 2001.

8. "Making a Market in Biometrics", The McLean Group. September 15, 1999. International Biometric Industry Association. *www.ibia.org*.

9. "The Biometric Industry Report, Market and Technology Forecasts to 2003", Elsevier Advanced Technology.

10. Round Three Comparative Biometric Testing for IT Security and E-Commerce. Final Report August 2001. International Biometric Group. *www.biometricgroup.com*.

11. World Biometric Market. June 2001. Frost and Sullivan. *www.frost.com*.

12. Lehman Brothers' 1999 Security Industry Overview: "Although the Biometric device industry may be less than USD 100 million today, we estimate that this market will grow 30-35 % annually to reach USD 400 million in five years."

13. James E. Bauer, Deputy Assistant Director, Office of Investigations, US Secret Service: "Ready or not, here it comes: Identity Take Over Fraud has come into its own, and promises not to go away until significant changes evolve in the manner and methods by which personal identifiers are collected and used. Consumers would do well to arm themselves with knowledge on how to mend damages when victimised."

14. BBC, 16 November 2003: "Identity fraud is a 21st century crime. It is silent, hidden, difficult to investigate and breathtakingly simple".

15. Rapport d'étude qualitative, SOFRES, July 2002: "La carte d'identité électronique : perception et attentes".

16. "Biometrics and the 'Financial Services Modernisation Act of 1999'", IBIA. CardTech/SecurTech 2000, Miami Beach, 3 May 2000.

17. Commission nationale de l'informatique et des libertés: 23rd Activities Report, 2002.

18. Draft, US Department of Defense and Federal Biometric System Protection Profile for Medium Robustness Environments (Version 0.02, 3 March 2002).

Bibliography

Articles and Reports

DIDIER, Bernard and Francis WEISS (2003), "La biométrie, nouvel outil stratégique de souveraineté", *Revue Défense Nationale*, November.

DIDIER, Bernard (2003), "Moyens et technologies de détection et d'alertes sur les attaques de la chaîne de confiance identitaire", Conseil Scientifique de la Défense, Confidential Report, October.

Lectures and Presentations

OFFICE PARLEMENTAIRE D'ÉVALUATION DES CHOIX SCIENTIFIQUES ET TECHNOLOGIQUES, "Les méthodes scientifiques d'identification des personnes à partir de données biométriques et les techniques de mise en œuvre" by M. Christian Cabal, Député. Record of Hearings (Bernard Didier et al.).

DIDIER, Bernard and Samuel HAILU CROSS (2003), "Biometric Management of Institutional Titles: Securing Passports and Visas", Salon Cartes, Paris, November.

DIDIER, Bernard (2001), "Brèves introductions sur le marché du traitement automatique de l'empreinte digitale", CNIL International Conference.

DIDIER, Bernard (2001), "Identification et biométrie", Journées Sciences et Défense.

DIDIER, Bernard (2002), "À propos de biométrie...", Club CSA, Paris, December.

Market Studies

Worldwide Hardware and Biometrics Authentication Forecast and Analysis, 2001–2006, published by IDC.

The Biometric Industry Report – Forecasts and Analysis to 2006 – Second Edition, Elsevier Advanced Technology, 2002.

Biometric Report 2003–2007, International Biometric Group.

MSI Study: "Le marché du contrôle d'accès électronique en France", MSI Marketing Research for Industry Ltd., August 2002.

Biometrics and the Automotive Industry, Frost and Sullivan, 2002.

Biometrics in Smart Cards, Frost and Sullivan, 2002.

Biometrics in Travel, Frost and Sullivan 2002.

World Biometrics Equipment Market, Frost and Sullivan, 2002.

BIOVISION Final Report, October 2003. Fifth Framework IST programme, European Commission.

ISBN 92-64-10772-X
The Security Economy
OECD 2004

Chapter 4

RFID: The Concept and the Impact

by
Steve Hodges and Duncan McFarlane
Auto-ID Lab, Cambridge University
United Kingdom

1. Introduction

Radio frequency identification, or RFID, has sprung into prominence in the last five years with the promise of providing a relatively low-cost means for connecting nonelectronic objects to an information network. In particular, the retail supply chain has been established as a key sector for a major deployment of RFID technology. This chapter provides a background to the technology and its position with regard to competing technologies. A range of applications is reviewed and the chapter concludes with some comments on the likely societal impact of RFID and potential barriers to deployment. The report is aimed at a nontechnical audience – namely, senior staff from a spectrum of areas including insurance, banking, telecommunications, government institutions and academia. It does not cover any technologies other than RFID, and in particular does not address technologies that may be candidates for tracking people.

2. Technology

This section reviews the background to and operations of RFID systems (Finkenzeller, 1999). It also reviews the networking implications of having ubiquitous RFID data available and finally contrasts RFID to other comparable technologies.

Introduction to RFID systems

At its most simple, a radio frequency identification system consists of two components, namely a tag (also called a transponder) and a reader (also called an interrogator). The tag is designed to be small and cheap – perhaps the size of a credit card or smaller – while the reader is more expensive and larger, typically about the size of a laptop computer (Figure 1). The RFID tag contains a small amount of memory for holding data, and whenever that tag comes into proximity with the RFID reader, the reader will detect the tag's presence and can read its data.

A real-world RFID application will usually employ many RFID tags, which are attached to physical objects. When one of these objects comes into proximity with the RFID reader, data from the associated tag can be read; the data may be used to identify that specific object or to provide information about it. Similarly, real applications of the technology often make use of several RFID readers, so that the tagged objects can be identified in different locations.

Figure 1. **Examples of an RFID tag and different types of reader**

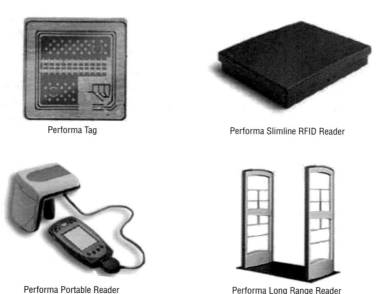

| Performa Tag | Performa Slimline RFID Reader |
| Performa Portable Reader | Performa Long Range Reader |

Note: Manufactured by Checkpoint Systems (a). Real size of the tag (top left) is around 5 cm by 5 cm. The Slimline reader (top right) is around 35 cm by 25 cm.

There are many different types of RFID system that vary in their exact mode of operation and operating performance. With "active" RFID systems, the tag contains a small battery that enables it to control communication with the reader. A completely "passive" RFID tag, on the other hand, has no battery but instead harvests power for its operation from the reader's radio communication signal. This means that the reader has to drive communication, but that makes the tag much cheaper.

How RFID operates

RFID relies on radio frequency communication. The reader emits energy in the form of a radio wave at a particular frequency, which is used to power and to communicate with the tags. As the radio waves propagate through the environment, their energy gradually dissipates – so that a tag beyond a certain distance from the RFID reader will not be able to pick up enough signal to operate reliably. In other words, the maximum operating distance between the RFID reader and tag (also known as the range) is limited. The exact range depends on a great many factors, including the radio frequency being used for communication, the power emitted by the reader, sources of radio interference and objects in the environment that are likely to reflect or absorb radio waves. A typical range for a passive RFID system will be anywhere between a few centimetres and a few metres. If a battery is incorporated into the tag, the range is increased dramatically, to many dozens of metres or more.

Since the communication mechanism is based on radio wave propagation, there is no need for a direct "line of sight" between the reader and the tag. (Contrast this with barcode systems, where the reader must be able to "see" the barcode label.) This means that tagged objects may be identified even if the tag or even the entire object is not in direct view of the reader – they may, for example, be inside packaging or hidden behind other objects. Also, most modern RFID systems can identify multiple tags in very quick succession (from tens to hundreds per second). This means that many tagged objects can be read in effect simultaneously as they pass by an RFID reader, something not easily achievable with other technologies such as barcodes. Although the relative orientation of the tag and the reader does alter the operating range to some extent, it is often possible to set up an RFID system so that this effect is not important – in other words, tagged objects may pass by a reader with little constraint on their orientation or alignment, another big advantage over many other identification technologies.

RFID systems rely on the use of a radio communication channel for their operation. This has a number of implications relating to the security of system operation. The most fundamental consideration is that the channel is, by its very nature, shared within any given vicinity.

This means that:

● Any transmissions that occur may be detected by any other equipment within range.

● Any other equipment may also make transmissions – which will potentially interfere.

The former of these two observations is often considered to constitute a significant security risk – especially given that the system operates without line of sight, which may make it relatively easy for an eavesdropper to remain hidden. However, the signals that emanate from the tag are incredibly weak, so an eavesdropper would need to be quite close by (certainly no further from the tag than the genuine reader). It is possible to design an RFID system that uses completely secure communications, where the information that is communicated is encrypted, but this will impact the cost of the tags and the performance of the system (range, communication speed, etc.) and is not currently seen to be commercially viable.

The latter of the two issues above is perhaps more interesting. For one thing, it means that an unauthorised reader is at liberty to communicate with tags. But it also means that any equipment that generates radio communication signals at the same operating frequency as the RFID system will interfere with the RFID operation, reducing performance and potentially rendering it inoperable. This is unlikely to occur by chance – it would mostly likely be due to the malicious (and illegal) operation of interfering equipment.

History and current state of the art

The concepts behind RFID were first discussed in the mid- to late 1940s, following on from technical developments in radio communications in the 1930s and the development of radar during the Second World War (Roberti, 2002). An early published work exploring RFID is the landmark paper by Harry Stockman (1948), "Communication by Means of Reflected Power". Stockman stated then that "[e]vidently, considerable research and development work has to be done before the remaining basic problems in reflected-power communication are solved, and before the field of useful applications is explored."

The 1950s were an era of exploration of RFID techniques; several technologies related to RFID were developed, such as the long-range transponder systems of "identification, friend or foe" (IFF) for aircraft (Landt and Catlin, 2001). A decade of further development of RFID theory and applications followed, including the use of RFID by the US Department of Agriculture for tracking the movement of cows. In the 1970s the very first commercial applications of the technology were deployed, and in the 1980s commercial exploitation started to increase, led initially by small companies.

In the 1990s RFID became much more widely deployed but in vertical application areas, which resulted in a number of different proprietary systems being developed by the different RFID solutions providers. Each of these systems had slightly different characteristics (primarily relating to price and performance) that made them suitable for different types of application. However, the different systems were incompatible with each other – e.g. tags from one vendor would not work with readers from another. This significantly limited adoption beyond the niche vertical application areas – the interoperability needed for more widespread adoption could not be achieved without a single standard interoperable specification for the operation of RFID systems. Such standardisation was also needed to drive down costs.

The drive towards standardisation started in the late 1990s. There were a number of standardisation efforts, but the two successful projects were:

● The ISO 18000 series of standards (AIM Global Website) that essentially specify how an RFID system should communicate information between readers and tags.

● The Auto-ID Centre specifications (Auto-ID Centre Website) on all aspects of operation of an RFID asset-tracking system, which has subsequently been passed onto EAN.UCC (the "custodians" of the common barcode) for international standardisation.

It is quite possible that these two standards will merge in the future to create one single specification of interoperable RFID system operation, which will promote larger-scale adoption of the technology and help to drive down costs. This means that passive RFID tags and readers, which in the past cost in the region of USD 0.50-1.00 and USD 1 000-2 000 respectively, are now heading towards USD 0.05-0.10 and USD 200-400. The RFID automated identification system specifications being developed by the Auto-ID Centre (Website) have focused on establishing global, open specifications for very low-cost tags and readers. This is discussed more in the next section.

The Auto-ID Centre

The Auto-ID Centre is a university-based organisation that was formed in 1999, initially by MIT, the UCC (Uniform Code Council, the barcode "custodians" in North America), Gillette, and Procter & Gamble. The motivation of the Centre was to develop a system suitable for tracking consumer packaged goods as they pass through the supply chain in order to overcome problems of shrinkage and poor on-shelf availability of some products. The Centre quickly expanded; by October 2003 it had over 100 member companies, all with a common interest in either deploying the technology in their organisations or in supplying the technology components.

Early on in the life of the Centre, it became clear that RFID would form a cornerstone of the technological solution, and with the help of some end-user and technology companies the Centre was instrumental in driving down the cost of RFID to the point where adoption became cost-effective in some application areas. Part of the solution to keeping costs down is a single-minded drive to reduce RFID tag complexity, and one approach to this advocated by the Auto-ID Centre is to store as little data about products as possible actually on the tag. Instead, this information is stored on an organisation's computer network, which is much more cost-effective. Hence, an RFID-based Auto-ID system generally comprises the following elements:

1. A unique identification number which is assigned to a particular item (the so-called electronic product code, or EPC).

2. An RFID tag that is attached to the item and is capable of storing – at a minimum – a unique identification number. The tag is capable of communicating this number electronically.

3. Networked RFID readers and data processing systems that are capable of collecting signals from multiple tags at high speed (hundreds per second) and of preprocessing this data in order to eliminate duplications and misreads.

THE SECURITY ECONOMY – ISBN 92-64-10772-X – © OECD 2004

4. One or more networked databases that store the product information.

With this approach, the cost of installing and maintaining such systems can be spread across several organisations while each is able to extract its own specific benefits from having uniquely identified items moving in, through, and out of its operations.

Comparison with other technologies

The most obvious technology that is comparable to RFID for many application areas is barcoding. Both these technologies involve the addition of a "tag" or "label" to an item that contains information about that item which allows it to be identified by a computer system.

A system designed to identify objects based on RFID tags has three main advantages over conventional barcode systems:

1. Barcodes are fixed once they have been created, whereas the data contained within an RFID tag can be augmented or changed as appropriate (Halliday). This means that:

   - It is possible to separate the time at which an object is tagged from the time at which information is stored on the tag – it may be advantageous, for example, to apply the tag at some point in an item's manufacturing process, before the information to be associated with the tag is known. This is not possible with a barcode.

   - Information can be updated as a tagged item moves through a process, keeping the important information with the tag (and the item) and so making it available at any point in its life (Halliday).

2. Barcodes have to be scanned deliberately by a person in a process that is difficult to automate. RFID tags, on the other hand, can be readily scanned automatically without human involvement. This means that:

   - The data can be obtained continuously and thus they are more up-to-date than data obtained only at specific intervals (like inventory counts) or specific points in the supply chain (like shipping or receiving).

   - Not involving a human in the process means that the readings can be less expensive and generally more accurate – incremental readings are virtually cost-free once the system has been installed. It also means that there may be fewer misreads.

   - Speed – many tags can be read simultaneously rather than having one read at a time.

3. Barcodes require line-of-sight to read, while RFID tags can be read (in any orientation) as long as they are within the reader's range. This implies that:

- The content of various conveyances (such as trailers, cases, pallets, shopping carts) can be read automatically without opening and sorting the conveyance.

- Barcodes do not work well when exposed to weather elements, when dirty, or if damaged in any way that interferes with clear line-of-sight reading. RFID is much more suited to operation in harsh environments (Halliday). The RFID tag can be hidden from view if this is beneficial, whereas a barcode is very obvious.

There are a number of other technologies in addition to RFID and barcoding that may be used in similar ways for storing information with an object or for identifying that object. These include magnetic stripe and contact systems, where information is stored on a magnetic stripe or in a chip (accessed by electrical contacts), and also computer vision systems that identify objects based on their visual appearance. The relative merits of all these different technologies are summarised in Table 1 below.

Table 1. **A comparison of RFID and other identification and data carrying technologies**

Characteristic	Tagging technology					
	Passive RFID	1-D barcode	2-D barcode	Magnetic stripe	Contact memory	Vision systems
Data capacity	High	Low	Medium	Low	High	Low
Data nature	Re-writeable	Read only	Read only	Re-writeable	Re-writeable	Read only
Human visibility/readability	Hidden	Visible, may be readable	Visible	Stripe visible	Contacts visible	No specific tag
Simultaneous identification	Yes	No	No	No	No	Possibly
Robustness	High	Medium	Low	Medium	Medium	
Operating distance	High	Medium	Medium	Low	Low	High
Line of sight needed?	No	Yes	Yes	No	In effect	Yes
Problematic objects (e.g. metal)	Yes	No	Not	Yes	Possibly	Yes (hard to see)
Tag cost	€ 0.1-1	< € 0.01	< € 0.01	< € 0.1	€ 0.1-1	€ 0 (n/a)
Reader cost	High	Low	Medium	Low	Low	Very high

3. Applications

This section provides an insight into the nature of the applications that have attracted RFID deployment to date, and also provides a window into future uses. As emphasised earlier, this review focuses solely on the application of tags to inanimate objects.

THE SECURITY ECONOMY – ISBN 92-64-10772-X – © OECD 2004

Applications: past, present and planned

Direct sensing of product identity is important in environments where it is too complex, uncertain or expensive to extract information about product movement via indirect methods; generally these involve computer tracking models and proximity sensing devices. Following the contrast between barcoding and RFID systems in Section 2, it is clear that when an easily automated, wireless, non-line-of-sight system is required and where multiple simultaneous reads are preferred, RFID has significant attractions.

These characteristics are reflected in applications of RFID to date, such as supply chain management; anti-theft systems, electronic tolling, facilities management (*e.g.* libraries); airline baggage handling and asset tracking. The table below compares the nature of these different applications, indicating that in many ways supply chain applications are – at least at present – rather different to most other existing applications.

Table 2. **Summary of the characteristics of different RFID applications**

	Tolling	Library	Asset	Airline	EAS	Supply chain
Complexity of the information on tag	M	L	H	L	L	L
Single or multiple applications for each tag	S	S	S	S	S	M
Volume of tags	L	L	L	M	M	H
Expected life of tag	H	H	H	M	M	L

This difference highlights the impact of the Auto ID Centre's work which has shifted the paradigm of RFID from low-volume, high-cost applications to those where high volume is critical, where costs must be as low as possible and benefits from a single tag must be achieved across multiple applications. The following table indicates the range of applications potentially achievable across the retail supply chain in which reduction of variables and uncertainties is of prime importance.

More detailed case studies

The short application "case studies" below will provide insight into the way that RFID solutions are being deployed. These are intended to be illustrative but not comprehensive.

Table 3. **Potential RFID applications across the retail supply chain**

Supply chain area	Description	Variables/uncertainties	RFID applications
Shipping	Shipment consolidation, contract compliance, routing optimisation, tendering and other transportation management functions associated with getting shipments out the door	Late orders, emergency shipments, lack of transportation capacity, lack of inventory visibility for order completion, misplaced and mis-picked items, etc.	Upstream visibility increasing planning options, simplified optimisation of trailer contents, speeding loading processes
Transportation process	All the processes and activites performed by the carrier, logistics company or whomever, in connection with the transportation process	Delays, misrouted packages in terminal operations, last-minute diversion of conveyances, dynamic trucking operations, wrong drop-off and pick-up operations, pilferage during transit, spoilage, etc.	Increased speed, simplicity and accuracy in tracking: order tracking, sub-conveyance tracking of part loads/individual pallets, speeding of tracking of individual items
Receiving process	Verification, acknowledgement, pairing and put-away activities associated with receiving shipments at the buyer location	Item shortages, wrong items, wrong quantities, deliveries to the wrong location (or receiving door within a location), put-away in wrong locations, wrong data entry, etc.	One touch verification, automated proof of delivery processing, accurate/fault-tolerant locating of items
Internal processes	Includes all the processes taking place within the buyer's facility. These may include transformation in a factory, storage in a warehouse, display in a store and all the processes around these activities	Errors in determining product state during processing, quality problems, raw material stockouts, inventory mismatches, unknown location of product within the facility, etc.	Manufacturing: raw material, sub-assembly tracking, asset tracking Warehousing: inventory management, spare part management Retail: shelf-level monitoring, automated reordering, auto checkout

Inventory control

Companies are starting to use RFID technology for warehouse applications that range from inventory counting of tagged products to product location and picking.

Figleaves, a UK online retailer of ladies' underwear, tags totes with RFID transponders and places readers in bays, so workers can correctly identify the location of a particular tote (Eurotag Newsletter, 2003). The system saves the company time and labour in not having to double-check orders before shipping. The system enables staff to pick 60 000 items a month with an error rate of less than 0.1%. But they would like to eliminate *all* failed picks by also using RFID to make sure bins are where they are supposed to be. Today, if a bin is not in the right location, it is very hard to find because it could be almost anywhere in the facility. Figleaves hopes to install tags on shelf edges and on the bins that carry products, and even on all items in a bin when the cost of tags drops further. That way, staff could stroll through the warehouse, scan the shelves with a handheld scanner

Figure 2. **An RFID-enabled library system**

Source: Landt and Catlin, 2001.

and make sure every bin is in the right location. Thus when staff pulled up with a cart, they would be virtually guaranteed to find the right product right away. Figleaves have established a business case for item-level tagging provided the tag price falls below USD 0.10.

Grocery distributor Associated Food Stores in Salt Lake City uses an RFID-based, real-time locating system at its distribution centre (Violino, 2004). The system enables Associated managers to know when trucks enter or leave the distribution yard and their exact location. RFID also can measure certain performance levels, such as detecting an increase in temperature that would indicate a refrigerator truck door was left open.

Library systems

RFID technology is well-suited to material management in a library setting. RFID tags can easily be incorporated into books and other library media. The tags may be applied at source (at the time of publishing) or after manufacturing, *e.g.* by the library staff as items are acquired.

The self-checkout system developed by Checkpoint (Checkpoint Systems Inc. b, c) allows patrons of the library to check out materials themselves, saving staff time and providing privacy. All types of library cards can be used, including those using traditional barcodes, magnetic strips or smartcards. Receipts are provided automatically. A user-friendly touch screen monitor guides the patron through the checkout process. Sensors automatically guard the library entrances and exits. They constantly query materials that pass through the sensors for proper checkout. Materials are verified against the library circulation system. If a person attempts to steal books, the system can alert staff. It is also possible to identify stolen items should they later be returned, and to highlight items that need to be replaced. A portable hand-held wand can be used to inventory materials in a library very quickly, and can assist in the location of mis-shelved materials.

Toll collection

Electronic payment systems enabled by RFID technology are becoming increasingly popular for road toll collection. An RFID tag (typically an active or semi-passive tag) is carried by the vehicle and a reader is deployed at each toll collection point. Whenever a tagged vehicle passes through a collection point it can be detected and identified, and this information is used to levy the appropriate charge for the journey, electronically. The advantages of electronic tolling are clear from the driver's point of view – there is no need to slow down significantly at the toll booths, no need to have the correct change to hand, no queuing. Similarly, costs of collecting tolls are significantly reduced by reducing staffing levels, cash handling and so on.

Tagging in the automotive industry

Enormous efforts in the automobile industry are devoted to ensuring that the tracking and traceability of all parts are in place for warranty purposes. Applications are being developed for tagging of car bodies (even at extremes of temperature), metallic parts, seats and tyres. The latter two are examined below for illustration.

Working with the Automotive Industry Action Group, Intermec (2002) has developed a UHF read/write tag that can be placed inside a car tyre and includes a unique serial number and a US Department of Transport coding number. The two numbers together can point to the exact location, time and conditions of manufacture of the tyre. The tag is placed during the manufacture of the tyre and is written to at the point of manufacture before distribution.

The tagging of car and truck seats is also receiving significant attention:

Johnson Controls (Collins, 2003) has deployed a 13.56 MHz tagging solution from Escort Memory Services for tagging all pallets used to convey the car and truck seats they produce. This was done primarily to improve tracking errors, specifically errors in delivery sequence and content for customers such as Daimler Chrysler, Ford Motor Co. and General Motors. RFID was chosen because of the harsh environments and the need to have very accurate identity readings. Barcodes were considered unsuitable because of line-of-sight restrictions and the likely replacement requirements over the pallet life. This is despite the USD 60 cost to place four tags onto each pallet at the tome. Most interestingly, Johnson has been able to use this same system as a means of improving processing procedures in their own production plant. Their production lines are inherently flexible in terms of dealing with small batches of multiple product types. However, limitations in material handling systems require the generation of inventory at the end of production that in the past has led to the mixing of orders of seats with slightly different specifications. The company can now produce multiple types of seats on a single production line without fear of confusion arising, and hence not only deliver but also produce to order in a flexible, just-in-time manner.

A wide range of RFID solutions have been developed specifically for this industry – which is in many ways the leader in the field, primarily because of the combination of relatively high volumes and high item prices that provides an attractive business justification for both the end-user and the solution developer.

Potential future applications

In addition to offering improvements in many existing processes, Auto ID systems will in the future enable fundamentally new service and business offerings that may have widespread ramifications. While the applications discussed so far are primarily based on a cost reduction justification, future applications might rather be seen as value adding. It is emphasised that the following discussion is in part speculative, and is simply intended to outline examples of fundamentally new applications being considered.

Retail stores of the future

The "holy grail" in retail is to reduce customer queues at checkout without increasing staffing levels. Many retailers are exploring options for "checkout free" stores, in which RFID scanners either in doorways or on board trolleys provide a self-checkout service that is hassle-free to the customer. Also, continuous shelf inventory checking using RFID and the addition of more frequent replenishments mean that shelf space for each item can be reduced substantially while increasing the level of service and reducing out-of-stock levels. The result may be smaller supermarkets and other retail outlets while the number of SKUs offered remains constant.

Procter & Gamble in Ohio, Phillip Morris in New York State, Sainsbury's in the United Kingdom and MGI (Metro) of Germany have opened Future Stores as a means of demonstrating the type of facilities that might be expected in an RFID-enhanced retail outlet. Applications range from smart – anti-theft – shelves, to wireless and automated ordering systems, dynamic use by dates, and intelligent trolleys that scan items as they are collected and update an electronic shopping list accordingly. Personalised advertising systems have also been tried.

RFID systems in the home

One of the first applications in the home may be continuous inventory. RFID, however, may give a new generation of home appliances the ability to know their content and act on it. Such actions may include cooking (in the case of a microwave oven, reading instructions embedded in the food packaging); a refrigerator and a cupboard ordering automatically from a store when the inventory level reaches a predetermined reorder point; and a refrigerator or medicine cabinet letting the owner know about the expiration date of its contents.

Product visibility over the entire life cycle

Today the supply chain for retail goods effectively ends at point of sale. RFID can enable applications in the usage phase (*e.g.* in the home) and at the end-of-life phase (*e.g.* disposal/recycling/reuse application) through information preservation. Keeping product information by connecting the RFID-tagged product to a networked database infrastructure through the usage and disposal processes means that information about the item is known throughout its life cycle. Figure 3, derived from McFarlane and Sheffi (2003), illustrates the current typical information profile of items as they go through a supply chain. The networked RFID-enhanced case is shown by the dashed line in Figure 3.

Figure 3. **Product information content along the supply chain**

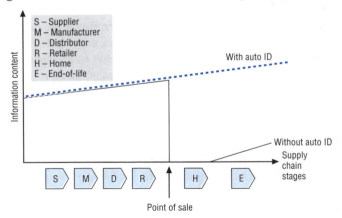

Source: Derived from McFarlane and Sheffi, 2003.

One of the benefits of the extension of the visibility into the home or workplace is in terms of more efficient end-of-life operations. Being able to detect which parts are contained, for example, in a discarded appliance and how that appliance was used at home can aid in the decision of where to send it for processing, allowing recycling centres to specialise. In the recycling centres RFID information can help automate the sorting process, which is the Achilles' heel of most recycling processes. It can help decide what parts to recycle, what can be used in remanufacturing, and what should be discarded and where.

4. Drivers and effects

Commercial drivers for RFID

A large number of consumer packaged goods (CPG) manufacturers and retailers have been exploring the potential benefits of RFID for tracking and identifying their products as they pass along the supply chain over a number of years. The most significant potential benefits of deploying such technology may differ from company to company. However, if a common, standardised, interoperable RFID system is deployed by all the trading partners in the supply chain, then the cost of deploying the technology can be amortised across the entire chain.

Recent technological developments in RFID that have brought down tag cost – especially in view of the very high volumes of tags that will be needed by the CPG industry. Coupled with recent progress in global standardisation, this means that RFID is now much more cost-effective in this application area. As a result, leading retailers are beginning to think very seriously about deploying the technology, and the world's largest retailer, Wal-Mart, has recently announced that by January 2005 its top 100 suppliers must use RFID technology to label all cases of products supplied. This requirement will be extended to all its suppliers in time. The so-called "Wal-Mart announcement" is incredibly significant given the size and power of Wal-Mart – it will clearly drive the adoption of RFID in the CPG supply chain.

The US Department of Defense has issued a similar mandate, relating to the RFID tagging of items that it purchases, and the leading UK retailer Tesco is already using RFID in one of its distribution centres and with some of its suppliers. Tesco plans to extend its deployment of RFID significantly over the coming year. These plans will also force the product manufacturers to deploy RFID, thereby driving adoption of the technology significantly.

Legislative drivers for RFID

In addition to commercial factors, legislation can also be a big technology driver. There are a number of areas in which new legislation may well drive the adoption of RFID in certain industries and for certain application areas.

The European Waste Electrical and Electronic Equipment (WEEE) Directive (Europa, 2002) became European law in February 2003, setting collection, recycling and recovery targets for all types of electrical products. The Directives must be implemented in European member states by August 2004, although there is an additional two-year period before full compliance must be demonstrated. Of particular relevance to RFID is the compulsory producer responsibility for financing the management of consumer electronic and electrical waste. This means that producers need to be able to identify the electronic and electrical equipment that they originally produced (because they will not want to incur the cost of disposing of another manufacturer's equipment). Also, they would benefit from being able to identify their own products accurately, in order to recycle the sub-components as effectively as possible. Similarly, the EU Directives on Packaging and Packaging Waste and the Management of End-of-life Vehicles Legislation place further pressures in the areas of packaging and motor vehicles.

Legislation regarding the tracking of medicines and foodstuffs in order to ensure human health and safety is another driver for the adoption of RFID technology. In some cases, existing or proposed legislation requires quite onerous audit trails of such products to be maintained by manufacturers and retailers. In these cases, while a number of different technologies might be used to meet the guidelines, RFID is an obvious choice for cost-effective implementation. However, in some instances RFID is being explicitly recommended or mandated. For example, the Healthcare Distribution Management Association (HDMA), a nonprofit organisation for distributors, has recently recommended that manufacturers and wholesalers of pharmaceutical drugs and other healthcare products begin putting RFID tags on cases in 2005 and deploy related infrastructure needed to take advantage of those tags (RFID Journal, 2003a). Additionally, in the food industry, food traceability enabled by RFID is a major topic for discussion (Food Traceability Report, 2003).

Social impact of RFID

This section briefly reviews the possible social impact of RFID, examining the individual, society as a whole and the environment.

Impact on the consumer

- *Consumer benefits* – Identified benefits to the consumer from RFID range from those in a retail store (reduced queuing, fresher goods, increased product availability), to the home (automated product checking, drug authenticity and dosage monitoring, home security systems) to travel (improved airport luggage management), to simpler access and borrowing systems for public services such as libraries. There has been little attempt thus far to quantify the benefits of RFID to the consumer, as much of the industrial focus recently has been in the business supply chain, and in the media on concerns over potential privacy infringements (see below).

● *Consumer privacy concerns* – RFID has received a lot of attention in the worldwide press in recent months due to consumer privacy concerns, raised by a relatively small number of privacy advocates (Jha, 2003; Dodson, 2003). While consumers are genuinely concerned, in most cases the worries are based on a lack of understanding of exactly what the technology is capable of and how it can be used. The Auto-ID Centre has put forward a list of guidelines about best practice for addressing public concerns (RFID Journal, 2003b); these include visually marking products or packaging that contains an RFID tag, giving consumers the option to have the tag destroyed at the point of sale, and guaranteeing the anonymity of data collected regarding any tagged items.

Impact on society

● *Healthcare* – RFID developments for assisting hospital-based and in-home healthcare have the potential to improve quality, reduce the costs of hospital treatment and contribute significantly to the management of Europe's ageing population. Applications range from life cycle tagging of drugs (European Commission) to intelligent medicine cabinets that can check user ID and drug ID to ensure each is authorised appropriately.

● *Food safety* – The food tracing legislations discussed in the previous section are intended to secure the entire food chain and to ensure a safe and effective supply of foods to consumers, as well as the ability to trace and recall quickly and accurately if required.

Impact on the environment

● *Recycling and reuse of materials* – The legislative requirements in this area are discussed above. In addition, it is noted that the effective deployment of RFID in the end-of-life management of goods may in fact help these activities to become profitable, providing a positive feedback loop for further developments in the area.

● *Energy management* – The use of RFID-based circuitry in electrical goods is being explored within a EU research project as a means of monitoring and analysing the performance of equipment while in use (ELIMA). Data are extracted periodically and used to review energy consumption among other variables. Up to 50% of all energy expenditure on many electrical products over their life cycle occurs during their usage phase.

Potential barriers to success of RFID

Technological challenges include the following:

- *Data storage and access* – Tracking every object at the individual item level will generate enormous amounts of data that will have to be stored (probably using distributed databases) and accessed quickly. The Auto-ID Centre has developed migration strategies but this is done only at the cost of reducing the fidelity of the data.

- *Accuracy* – As operations and their underlying information systems grow to rely more and more on real-time, automated product identity data, the specifications placed on the identification system will tend towards absolute accuracy of the location information generated. This will place new challenges on the engineering and production of the tags and readers.

- *Interference* – With the proliferation of wireless devices (cordless and mobile phones, PDAs, consumer electronics devices, etc.), there is the potential for electromagnetic interference with RFID systems. This may be particularly important since RFID does not have its own dedicated frequency band in most jurisdictions, but rather operates in a band that is shared with other users.

- *IT integration* – Companies typically have a number of legacy IT systems. While some IT systems providers will have off-the-shelf solutions to address such implementation issues, it is likely that integration of RFID systems with existing systems may be difficult, time-consuming and expensive. The real-time nature of the item-level information that can be generated using an RFID system will place significant burden on the IT infrastructure.

- *Difficult-to-tag items* – The performance of an RFID system is very much dependent on the type of object being tagged and the environment in which that object needs to be identified. For example, objects with a high metal or liquid content typically absorb the RF energy emitted by a reader significantly, thereby reducing the range of an RFID system dramatically.

- *RF legislation* – RFID systems traditionally operate in regions of the radio spectrum that are unlicensed. This means that as long as the RFID reader follows some basic operating principles, it can be operated without the need for a special radio transmission licence. National governments are typically responsible for defining which parts of the radio spectrum are unlicensed and of these, which are suitable for RFID systems. Unfortunately, due to historical reasons, not all governments have the same allocations – North America, Europe, South Africa and Australia have slightly different allocations and operating principles, for example. Over time these differences are gradually being aligned, but this is a long-term process and in the shorter term there may be interoperability issues.

THE SECURITY ECONOMY – ISBN 92-64-10772-X – © OECD 2004

- *Recycling of tags* – If an RFID tag is truly embedded into an item (rather than attaching it to the packaging of the item, for example), then there may be an issue with subsequently recycling that item. The materials used to form the RFID tag (silicon chip, metallic antenna) may not be compatible with the recycling process for the item, thereby reducing the effectiveness of the recycling operation.

  Other challenges include:

- *Health and safety issues* – In the past, RFID reader deployment has not been particularly widespread. However, as this changes and workers and the general public increasingly come into contact with the technology, concerns about the health and safety impact of exposure to the radio waves generated by readers are likely to be raised. There is currently no evidence of potential harm to human health, but just as with exposure to mobile telephone radiation, it is important to continue to improve understanding in this area.

- *Criminal activity* – As technology in general develops, there is a trend away from physical operations and processes to electronic ones. One downside of this is that these operations and processes may become more open to abuse in certain respects. One example is the proliferation of unwanted "spam" email and computer viruses, which are transmitted relatively easily and cheaply through the electronic media that have replaced the physical communications mechanisms of previous generations. Similarly, it is possible to imagine scenarios where the electronic systems that rely on RFID-generated information to manage company operations may be abused to the detriment of that company. This might be due to malicious computer network traffic, or it could be due to intentional manipulation of the radio spectrum that prevents RFID information from being collected or even generates misleading RFID information (RFID Journal, 2003c). Such criminal activities might be motivated by an intellectual challenge (as with many computer viruses), by commercial gain or by terrorism.

- *The cost of RFID components* – RFID tags and readers will most likely continue to fall as the technology and the associated production processes improve. However, in the near term, costs are likely to limit adoption of the technology to the tagging of more expensive objects, such as pallets and cases of goods and higher-value items such as consumer electronics devices.

- *The cost of integration* – In addition to the direct deployment costs of RFID technology, there will be a big cost associated with IT systems integration. As indicated above, traditional IT systems are not designed to deal with the real-time generation of item-level information, and adding this capability will be costly.

5. Conclusion

This report has described the fundamentals of operation of radio frequency identification technology and the application areas in which such systems have traditionally been used. As the sophistication of the technology increases and the component costs drop, there will clearly be an increasing number of application areas in which the technology is cost-effective. Additionally, the standardisation of a number of aspects of RFID implementation means that systems deployed in different industries and by different companies will be interoperable, which further increases the cost-effectiveness of RFID deployment because the same infrastructure can be shared.

The most immediate expansion of RFID deployment is likely to be in the consumer packaged goods supply chain, so that product manufacturers, logistics companies and retailers can monitor the movement of goods much more accurately. By doing this, they hope to reduce shrinkage, mis-deliveries, diversion of goods and so on. The largest retailer in the world, Wal-Mart, are actively moving to RFID for this application on a very aggressive timescale, and are therefore driving their suppliers to adopt the technology too. Other retailers and government organisations are also moving in this direction, which will again drive adoption of RFID in the CPG supply chain.

Recent and planned legislative changes in a number of areas are likely to further drive adoption of RFID technology – either because the use of this specific technology is mandated or recommended, or because RFID is simply the most cost-effective way to comply with the new legislation. While there are factors that may act to slow the technology adoption, such as the concerns of consumers or the cost of systems integration, it currently looks like there will be a significant adoption in certain application areas in the relatively near term.

Bibliography

AIM GLOBAL WEBSITE, "JTC 1/SC 31 Automatic Identification and Data Capture Techniques", *www.aimglobal.org/standards/rfidstds/sc31.htm*.

AUTO-ID CENTRE WEBSITE, Archive, *www.epcglobalinc.org*.

CHECKPOINT SYSTEMS INC. (a), "Radio Frequency Identification (RFID) – Performa Commercial/Industrial Products", *www.checkpt.com/content/rfid/commperf.aspx*.

CHECKPOINT SYSTEMS INC. (b), "Radio Frequency Identification (RFID) Success Stories: Checkpoint Offers Proven RFID Solutions".

CHECKPOINT SYSTEMS INC. (c), "Checkpoint Intelligent Library System – Changing the Role of the Librarian".

COLLINS, Jonathan (2003), "Perfecting Just in Time Production", *RFID Journal*, November.

DODSON, Sean (2003), "The Internet of Things: A Tiny Microchip Is Set to Replace the Barcode on All Retail Items But Opposition Is Growing to Its Use", *The Guardian*, 9 October.

ELIMA – Environmental Life Cycle Information Management and Acquisition, EU Growth Programme 2001-3.

EUROPA (2002), "Activities of the European Union – Summary of Legislations, Waste Management".

EUROPEAN COMMISSION – JOINT RESEARCH CENTRE, "DRIVE – Drug in Virtual Enterprise", IST 12040.

EUROTAG NEWSLETTER (2003), "RFID Helps to Perfect Order Picking", April-June.

FINKENZELLER, K. (1999), "RFID Handbook", 1st Edition, Wiley and Sons Ltd.

"FOOD TRACEABILITY REPORT" (2003), *CRC Press*, LLC, Vol. 3, No. 4, March.

HALLIDAY, Steve, "But Can't Bar Codes Do Everything I Want?", High Tech Aid.

HODGES, Steve and Mark HARRISON (2003), "Demystifying RFID: Principles and Practicalities", Technical Report CUED/E-MANUF/TR-028, Cambridge University Engineering Department.

INTERMEC (2002), "Intermec Poised to Take the Fast Lane in RFID", *www.intermec.com/cgi-bin/ASP/*.

JHA, Alok (2003), "Tesco Ends Trial of CCTV Spy Chip on Razor Blades", *The Guardian*, 22 August.

LANDT, Jeremy and Barbara CATLIN (Transcore) (2001), "Shrouds of Time: The history of RFID", Published by AIM, the Association for Automatic Identification and Data Capture Technologies.

McFARLANE, D. and Y. SHEFFI (2003), "The Impact of Automatic Identification on Supply Chain Operations", *International Journal of Logistics*, Vol. 14, No. 1, pp. 1-17.

RFID JOURNAL (2003a), "RFID Touted for Drug Distribution", 10 November.

RFID JOURNAL (2003b), "Creating an RFID Privacy Plan", 26 May.

RFID JOURNAL (2003c), "RSA Security Designs RFID Blocker", 28 August.

ROBERTI, Mark (2002), "RFID: From Just-In-Time to Real Time", CIO Insight, 12 April.

STOCKMAN, Harry (1948), "Communication by Means of Reflected Power", Proceedings of the IRE (Institute of Radio Engineers), October, pp. 1196-1204.

VIOLINO, Bob (2004), "The Intelligent Warehouse", *RFID Journal*.

ISBN 92-64-10772-X
The Security Economy
OECD 2004

Chapter 5

Tracking by Satellite: GALILEO

by

René Oosterlinck
European Space Agency*

---

* The views expressed herein are the author's and do not necessarily reflect those of the European Space Agency.

In all aspects of our daily life – at home and at work, in industrial activities and at the level of nations – safety and security have become primary concerns.

Recommendations and actions have been proposed in many fields to provide a better response to those concerns worldwide. One such field is the use of satellites. In a category quite apart from telecommunication and earth observation satellites, which already play an important role in these issues, Global Navigation Satellite Systems (GNSS) could in the future be of strategic importance for safety and security.

The Global Navigation Satellite System

The advent of modern transportation went hand in hand with the need for quick and reliable navigation systems. A number of these were developed over the course of the 20th century; a few could provide navigation data irrespective of weather conditions and over a large part of the globe. These were ground-based radio navigation systems that used triangulation – with emitters beaming to known locations – as a means for positioning. (The LORAN system is a typical example.) The problem, of course, is that these emitters could only be placed on the surface of the earth, thereby limiting the coverage. Moreover, the position could only be two-dimensional; altitude could not be established, thereby excluding their use in aviation. A global tri-dimensional system called for satellite navigation. And, as the needs for such a system were first and foremost military, it was in that realm that the new global positioning system was introduced.

Global Navigation Satellite Systems – How does it work?

GNSS is based on three-dimensional triangulation. A constellation of satellites orbiting around the earth in a number of orbital planes (six for GPS, three planned for GALILEO) emits signals. These signals all contain an identification message indicating the satellite that is emitting the signal, an ephemeris table indicating the position of all operational satellites and – finally, and most importantly – the exact time the signal was emitted. When receiving the position of a single satellite, the receiver – through the use of the ephemeris table – knows the position of all other satellites at that given time.

The signals emitted by the satellites travel at the speed of light and will arrive at different times depending on the distance between receiver and satellite. Once a signal is received from a first satellite, the distance can be calculated. The receiver is thus located on the surface of a sphere whose radius is the distance between the satellite and the receiver; the satellite is the sphere's centre. When a second satellite is detected it too will define a sphere with itself as centre. The receiver is now located somewhere along the intersections of the two spheres, but the precise intersection point will only become clear with a third satellite and resulting third sphere.

In theory the signals stemming from three distinct satellites would be sufficient to determine the position of the receiver. That theory, however, hinges on the receiver's clock having the same accuracy as the one on board the satellites, which in practice is not the case. The time difference constitutes a fourth unknown; a fourth satellite will therefore be necessary to calculate the precise position of the receiver.

The accuracy of the system depends on a number of errors inherent in that system. The main errors are due to signals being delayed when traveling through the ionosphere and troposphere, the accuracy of the onboard clocks, background noise, and multi-path. Corrections are available to decrease these errors, e.g. ionosphere models (the effect of the ionosphere on the signals varies substantially from one place in the ionosphere to another), special design of the signals, etc. Very precise measurements are made through the use of local elements allowing accuracy at sub-centimetre level.

Global Positioning System (GPS)

The United States was the first with the implementation of a global positioning system with satellites. The first GPS satellite was launched in 1978, and very soon thereafter researchers realised that the GPS coarse and acquisition signal (C/A code) could be used for other purposes than just acquisition. Since this signal was not encrypted, anyone could use it. Many applications were developed, and these grew rapidly in importance and variety. Recognising the potential for civil applications, President Reagan announced that part of the GPS capabilities would be made available for civil use.

GPS thus officially offers two signals: one, highly accurate, is reserved for military purposes and is encrypted; a second is freely available for all users. Until recently this second signal was not fully reliable, since for purposes of selective availability a number of errors were deliberately introduced to limit misuse of the signal by "non-friendly" users. The errors were changed constantly, relaying false information regarding the time and position of the respective satellites. These errors considerably reduced the accuracy of the open access signal. On 1 May 2000 President Clinton announced that selective availability would be discontinued.

Though GPS is a military system, there has over recent years been a shift in GPS-related policy matters in the United States, with an increased emphasis on civil applications. This is illustrated by the law now in force on GPS, which comprises two main elements: sustainment and operation for military purposes and sustainment and operation for civilian purposes. The latter purposes include, in particular, standard positioning service for peaceful civil, commercial and scientific use on a continuous worldwide basis free of direct user fees.

GLONASS

The USSR also developed a military satellite navigation system, called GLONASS (GLObal NAvigation Satellite System). The constellation, now managed by Russia, has lost a lot of its original capacities. At present a very limited number of satellites are operational, and although there are plans to increase this number it is unlikely that those plans will be realised in the near future.

As conceived, the operational GLONASS constellation was composed of 24 satellites in three orbital planes, with a potential for global coverage.

The GALILEO Programme

The objective of GALILEO is to set up a European autonomous Global Navigation Satellite System (GNSS) that is highly accurate and interoperable with other existing systems, i.e. GPS and GLONASS. The European objective of full autonomy in satellite navigation will be achieved in a two-step approach, beginning with the European Geostationary Navigation Overlay Service (EGNOS) in 2004. Europe is building EGNOS as a complement to GPS and the Russian GLONASS to provide a civil service. EGNOS increases the accuracy of those two constellations and additionally includes a warning system in case of their malfunction (integrity).

GALILEO, the second step, will be the first civil satellite positioning and navigation system, designed and operated under public control. Its conception and architecture is therefore driven by a multitude of users and services. Special attention has been given to security aspects, with a view to protecting its infrastructure and avoiding the potential misuse of its signals.

The rationale for Europe to build GALILEO is threefold:

● *Strategic:* to protect European economies from dependency on other states' systems that could deny access to civil users at any time, and to enhance safety and reliability.

● *Commercial:* to secure an increased share for Europe in the equipment market, related technologies and value added services. In the future the role of GNSS will increase substantially; everyone worldwide will be able to use it on a daily basis, and many value added services will develop. A monopoly of one state may lead to misuse of that position, thereby weakening European industries' competitiveness.

● *Macroeconomic:* to deliver efficiency savings for industry, create social benefits through cheaper transport, reduced congestion and less pollution, and stimulate employment.

GALILEO – Architecture

GALILEO will be composed of a global component that will provide the Signals in Space required for satellite-only services. It will comprise a space segment, a ground segment and a number of service centres. The space segment comprises a constellation of 27 active satellites plus three spare satellites in Medium Earth Orbit, orbiting in three planes. The ground segment comprises a Ground Control System for the satellites in orbit and a navigation mission ground segment for the Signal in Space. The service centres provide information and warranty on the performances and data.

Figure 1. **Galileo's components and services**

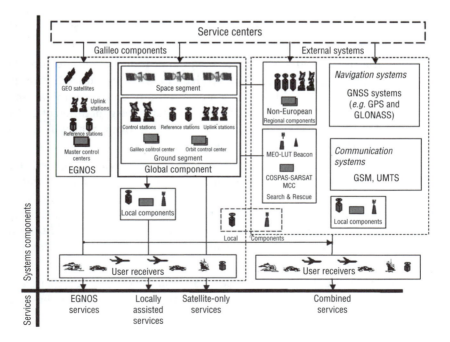

Regional components will complement the system. These will include ground segments incorporating terrestrial components across all regions of the world to provide integrity data, either up-linked directly from each region or routed to the ground segment of the global component for up-link.

Local components are also foreseen, to enhance the satellite-only services on a local basis through a combination of GALILEO signals and other GNSS or non-GNSS systems (*e.g.* GSM and UMTS). These local components will allow enhanced services at users' level and will enable development of a wide range of applications.

An independent yet interoperable system

GALILEO is being designed as an independent satellite navigation system, but one that can, as mentioned above, be used with other systems, notably GPS.

There are three main interoperability objectives:

- The first is to ensure GALILEO's interoperability at receiver level with other GNSS systems (mainly GPS). This is reflected in the study and choice of frequencies, signal structure, time reference frame, and geodetic data.

- In addition, interoperability with other non-GNSS systems, such as ground navigation systems or mobile communication networks, will be necessary to enable a reduction of GNSS deficiencies through the provision of combined positioning services.

- Finally, the use of GALILEO with telecommunication systems to provide joint navigation/communication services must be optimised. This is an additional functionality that enables enhanced communications capabilities (*e.g.* higher data transfer) and facilitates the generation of GNSS value-added services, such as location-based services, that will figure importantly in the future GNSS market.

Contrary to the actual GPS, which offers only one civil signal, GALILEO will offer a number of signals supporting four different navigation services and one service to support search and rescue operations. These services have been identified to cover the needs of the widest range of users, including professional users, scientists, mass-market users, and safety of life and publicly regulated domains. The following GALILEO satellite-only services will be provided worldwide:

- *The Open Service (OS)* makes available a combination of open signals free of user charge, and provides position and timing performances that are competitive with other GNSS systems.

Figure 2. **Open Service (OS)**

		Open Service (positioning)	
	Carriers	Single frequency	Dual-frequency[1]
Type of receiver	Computes integrity	No	
	Ionospheric correction	Based on simple model	Based on dual-frequency measurements
Coverage		Global	
Accuracy (95%)		H: 15 m V: 35 m	H: 4 m V: 8 m
Integrity	Alarm limit	Not applicable	
	Time-to-alarm		
	Integrity risk		
Availability		99.8%	

1. The performance of a service with the carriers is under assessment.

- *The Safety of Life Service (SoL)* improves the open service performances, providing timely warnings to the user when the system fails to meet certain margins of accuracy (integrity). It is envisaged that a service guarantee will be provided.

- *The Commercial Service (CS)* provides access to two additional signals, to allow for a higher data rate throughput and to enable users to improve accuracy. It is envisaged that a service guarantee will be provided.

- *The Public Regulated Service (PRS)* provides position and timing to specific users requiring a high continuity of service with controlled access. Two PRS navigation signals with encrypted ranging codes and data will be available.

Figure 3. **Public-Regulated Service (PRS)**

		Public-Regulated Service
	Carriers	Dual-frequency
Type of receiver	Computes integrity	Yes
	Ionospheric correction	Based on dual-frequency measurements
Coverage		Global
Accuracy (95%)		H: 6.5 m V: 12 m
Integrity	Alarm limit	H:20-V:35
	Time-to-alarm	10 s
	Integrity risk	$3.5 \times 10^{-7}/150$ sec
Continuity risk		$10^{-5}/15$ s
Timing accuracy w.r.t. UTC/TAI		100 nsec
Availability		99.5%

- *The Search and Rescue Service (SAR)* broadcasts globally the alert messages received from beacons emitting distress signals. It will help enhance the performances of the international COSPAS-SARSAT search and rescue system.

Safety and security applications

Around one hundred applications of GNSS have been identified, many of which are either already operational or in a pre-operational phase. It is expected that the list will further expand in the future once GALILEO is in operation.

GALILEO is essentially a positioning and timing system allowing a user to establish their precise position at any moment in time. As the system allows for dynamic positioning, it will be able to guide the user from one point to another.

However, GALILEO is not in itself a tracking system, with the exception of the search and rescue service. It is a one-way system whereby only the operator of the receiver knows where the user is. For many safety- and security-related applications this will not be sufficient; it will be mandatory that others also know the position or dynamic behaviour of the user. For these applications a combination of systems (*e.g.* communication) is thus essential.

Applications in the field of transport

As already mentioned, GNSS is a static and dynamic positioning system; it is thus not astonishing that the first and main applications are found in the field of transport (*i.e.* of almost all types – ground, air and maritime).

Road applications

The road applications include assistance for car-driving navigation, fleet management operations (*e.g.* taxis, trucks, buses), and vehicle guidance. Advance Driver Assistance will also include functions for safety and mobility improvements in road traffic, such as collision warning, vision enhancement, low-speed manoeuvring aid, etc.

With respect to safety and security, a very important application is efficient intervention in case of accidents. The response time for emergency services to reach the scene of an accident varies greatly. Currently the response depends on user contact by telephone or on infrastructure-based sensing equipment. When mobile phone calls are involved, the location of the accident or incident cannot be accurately determined in 40% of the cases.

Rapid response to emergencies is a critical requirement, on the one hand for saving lives and aiding the injured but also for the removal of obstructions and the maintenance of efficient traffic flow. Some domestic vehicles are now being equipped with automatic crash sensors and positioning systems that can communicate directly with emergency dispatch centres. Such systems require no action on the part of the driver; they communicate a vehicle's exact location even if he or she is incapacitated. In the absence of a central control station, emergency vehicles can be equipped with independent tracking systems enabling precision resource deployment. GALILEO will enhance the capabilities of such systems significantly, even specifying the lane in which an incident has occurred.

Another important application is the tracking and control of transport of hazardous goods. It would be possible in the future to follow on a continuous basis the transport of such goods through the combination of a GALILEO receiver installed on the truck and an emitter sending a signal to a local security authority. In case of problems the security authority could take immediate action, knowing exactly where the truck is located. In addition to the position of the truck, information on the characteristics of the hazardous goods could also be transmitted to the security authority. The system could moreover be equipped with a speed detector, which would inform the truck driver that his speed is above the limit, and simultaneously transmit the same information to the security authority.

The European Space Agency has developed a location-based service called EGNOS TRAN (Terrestrial Regional Augmentation Networks). The system comprises a service centre in Rome where the position of dangerous goods transport vehicles can be monitored. The service centre communicates via GPRS with the vehicle, which is equipped with an EGNOS receiver and can be assisted by the service centre with data messages and with EGNOS data when the EGNOS signal in space is temporarily lost due to the urban environment or a mountainous region, forest, etc.

Civil aviation

In the civil aviation domain, GALILEO will be used in the various phases of the flight, i.e. in en route guidance, airport approaches, landing (Cat I, II, and III), and for ground guidance. GALILEO will be highly beneficial where the classic ground infrastructure (i.e. surface movement radars) does not exist or is insufficient for increased air traffic.

Maritime

In the maritime area GALILEO will be used as an onboard navigation means for all forms of marine transport, including ocean and coastal navigation, port approach, and port manœuvres as well as fluvial transport.

Rail

The rail community will also benefit from GALILEO, with applications such as train control, train supervision, fleet management, track survey and passenger information service. The GALILEO joint undertaking has launched, under the 6th framework programme, a demonstration study (GADEROS). The study will explore the use of GNSS integrity and safety of life characteristics in defining a satellite-based system to perform train location for safe railway applications. These will be integrated into the European Rail Traffic Management System (ERTMS)/European Train Control System (ETCS).

Industrial applications

One area is civil engineering, where GALILEO will be used as the main survey tool, as well as for the continuous monitoring of structures (buildings, bridges, etc.).

A second area is monitoring the environment. The combination of specific environmental measurements – with GALILEO indicating the precise location associated with each measurement – will considerably increase the accuracy of detailed three-dimensional images of the seabed in ports, harbours and estuaries, on coasts and in the ocean for safe passage, and that of data for dredging applications.

A third area is geodesy: geodesists will use GALILEO receivers for the monitoring of geophysical phenomena, through the measurement of relative motion of fixed reference points; the geodetic sensors could also be interfaced with other equipment such as photogrammetric cameras, synthetic aperture radar and bathymeters.

Local-based services (LBS)

Local-based services (LBS) comprise all services where information on the location of the user is combined with an added value service.

A classical example is someone asking the way to the nearest hospital. The service provider compares the user's location with the location of the hospitals stored in their database. Then they indicate to the user the nearest hospital and the fastest route. The service may moreover provide guidance throughout the trip, up to the final destination. The service providers could also point customers to restaurants, movie theatres or parking lots. Until now several maps and guidebooks indicate the position of such places but that very often is not sufficient. Equally important is, first, knowing exactly where you are and, second, knowing how to get to your destination on a continuous basis.

There are many other applications under development apart from this example. One, very important, is assistance to disabled persons.

Personal navigation assistance for people with impaired vision

Map-reading for the blind at present depends largely on additional aid from sighted people. While tactile maps are helpful in giving an overview of a country, region or city, they are unable to detail streets and landmarks adequately. Until now, satellite orientation tools have also failed to accurately guide visually impaired people through the streets because signals are lost due to tall buildings and other obstacles; this can lead to incorrect positioning by up to 30 or 40 metres. GALILEO will allow a better coverage in urban areas and will help to provide an enhanced navigation service for the blind community. Through so-called "local elements", GALILEO will also improve and facilitate possibilities for indoor localisation.

A project supported by ESA has successfully proved the feasibility of such a system by using EGNOS, the precursor to GALILEO. A hand-held device speaks to the user like any navigation device in a car – but as it weighs less than one kilo, it can be carried over the shoulder. It can be used in two ways: to guide users to their destination or to tell them where they are as they walk. EGNOS ensures the required accuracy in routing and navigational assistance. The tool also includes a Braille keyboard and voice synthesiser as well as Internet access. This project can pave the way for GALILEO while demonstrating the benefit of enhanced GNSS performances for these applications.

Assistance to Alzheimer's sufferers with memory loss

Many Alzheimer's sufferers, in the early stage of their illness, are still pursuing regular activities such as working, driving or shopping. A personal digital assistant (PDA), programmed with information about their habits and regular destinations, can help them stay integrated in their environment and cope with recurring problems. Such a device would have a simple interface where the user would only need a click on a picture of their desired destination, and a directional arrow would appear on the screen to point them in the right direction. The device could also suggest destinations based on criteria such as the current time and the user's exact location and direction provided by GALILEO. An Alzheimer's patient lost in a parking lot could use the device to find their car. Another might use it to find the stop where he usually takes the bus.

Personal protection and emergency calls

Mobile phones with an integrated GALILEO receiver will make it possible to precisely and immediately locate callers who have only a vague idea – or none whatsoever – of their locations. Responses to distress calls can thus be much quicker. This concept is part of Europe's development of the E-112 emergency call programme.

ESA is developing, in the frame of EGNOS TRAN, a personal protection application. The user interfaces with a service centre located in Rome through a PDA equipped with AGPS cell guide and GPRS SIMcard. The service localises the person upon request or in automatic mode. The user sends the GPS raw data and the service centre, which tracks the EGNOS signal in space, combines EGNOS data with the user data to compute an EGNOS position. The location is thereby determined within a few metres' accuracy and assistance can be organised rapidly if needed.

Disaster monitoring and prediction

A major objective of civil protection is to provide better protection for people, the environment and property against disasters. This includes supporting disaster monitoring. GALILEO can help monitor precursor events of some types of disasters, thereby optimising reaction time. For instance, in areas prone to flooding, the water level and dyke movements are usually monitored. GALILEO's accuracy, enhanced locally, will improve this monitoring. Earthquake prediction and volcano monitoring will be improved through timely information and warning.

Optimising disaster relief operations

Fire brigades will be supported by GALILEO in their fleet management. In urban environments, providing navigation and knowledge of the traffic situation can significantly improve fleet efficiency. Monitoring the position of the various vehicles involved in relief activities will allow better co-ordination of operations, especially when – in large-scale disasters – several different services are in place. Appropriate management of resources and personnel during emergency operations will increase their effectiveness and the safety of rescue teams. Each operator's position could be monitored, and tailored instructions formulated and communicated at a distance. The planned extended availability of GALILEO in difficult environments, including indoors, makes it suitable for this important application.

Cutting response times is a key factor for maximising success. This is more difficult in major disasters, where real-time (and continuing) resource monitoring is essential. GALILEO provides the required accuracy and reliability.

Flying helicopters in emergency operations usually involves very specific flight operation procedures, which require accurate and very demanding navigation capabilities. Here again, the high accuracy and reliability of GALILEO is particularly beneficial, making it an essential element. Helicopter landings in difficult environments, remote areas or on the roof of a hospital could be ably assisted by GALILEO, which could at the same provide information to a co-ordination centre for optimising the operations.

Law enforcement and liability issues

In order to avoid misuse of the system, or to use it in law enforcement or liability cases, it is mandatory that the signals received by the users not be jammed or spoofed and are reliable. For that reason, the commercial signal will be encrypted and provided with an integrity and authentication message. To use these assets the receiver must be certified, which entails the use of a private key cryptography. The GALILEO signals would contain an authentication message that would need to be decrypted by the receiver. Only messages with authentication would be used; the others would be automatically rejected. The "integrity" message would indicate the level of accuracy of the system.

A specific signal (service), PRS, is foreseen for governmental use. The need for the Public-Regulated Service results from the analysis of threats to the GALILEO system and the identification of infrastructure applications where disruption to the Signal in Space by economic terrorists, malcontents, subversives or hostile agencies could result in damaging reductions in national security, law enforcement, safety or economic activity within a significant geographic area.

PRS will provide a higher level of protection against these threats than is available from other services. Its objective is to improve the probability of continuous availability of the Signal in Space, in the presence of interfering threats, to well-identified users and well-identified receivers controlled by key management. A number of applications have been retained for the elaboration of the user requirements of the PRS. The major applications are at European-level law enforcement (e.g. EUROPOL, Transport Policy Regulations, Customs, OLAF) and peacekeeping forces. In addition, the PRS may serve special applications in individual member states deemed of strategic national interest.

The Public-Regulated Service signals will be broadcast on separate frequencies with respect to other GALILEO satellite-only services, so as not to lose the PRS when the other services are denied locally. They are wide-band signals resistant to involuntary interference or malicious jamming, and therefore offer a better continuity of service.

Conclusion

A number of value added services will be created through GALILEO, in particular in the field of safety and security. These services will be very powerful and save many lives and goods. They could, on the other hand, be seen as too powerful and may lead to misuse. Measures must therefore be developed for avoiding the "Big Brother is watching you" temptation – but that is another story.*

* See in particular Dee Ann Divis, "Saving Private Location", GPS World, 1 October 2003.

ISBN 92-64-10772-X
The Security Economy
OECD 2004

Chapter 6

Security Products:
Inside the Italian Electronic Identity Card

by

Alfio Torrisi

Stationery Office and Government Mint

and

Luigi Mezzanotte

L.C. Sistemia

Italy

Overview

Today, governments are increasingly using telecommunication networks and IT systems in order to effectively supply new services to citizens. This dramatically reduces bureaucracy costs while improving the quality of service.

Following months of meetings and studies, the actors involved finally and formally introduced a new concept in the Italian Official Gazette No. 169, dated 21 July 2000. The Italian Electronic Identity Card (EIC, or CIE in Italian) was designed to offer Italian citizens new levels of service and security in their interaction with all levels of government – national, regional and municipal. This electronic document attempts to satisfy simultaneously the goals of the e-government plan and the need to facilitate the relationship between citizens and the public administration. The government has officially entrusted the card's production to the Italian Stationery Office and Government Mint (IPZS – Istituto Poligrafico e Zecca dello Stato S.p.A.).

As to the technology involved, the Italian Government chose a hybrid solution – smart/optical – as the ID card platform, drawing on both IC chip and optical memory technologies.

The IC chip – well known in Europe for certifying online transactions – controls access to "e-government" services. It is conceived to allow electronic identification and authentication through network communication and to enable National Services links (CNS). The optical memory band, the most widely used advanced card technology for government ID programmes, ensures the strongest counterfeit resistance, data integrity and authentication, both machine-readable and visual. Finally, it guarantees permanent tracing of card issue and updating history, as well as multi-service provisions, through a large memory capacity.

The production, initialisation, personalisation and issuance of a secure, multi-application, multi-technology card demands the highest levels of security and control. This is especially critical with a card issuance system involving up to 8 000 local communities.

Goals

The goals that the EIC is expected to achieve are: 1) *security*, for the complete life cycle of the card – production, emission and user phase – serving as a physical identity document; 2) *service provision*, to secure electronic

THE SECURITY ECONOMY – ISBN 92-64-10772-X – © OECD 2004

identification, authentication and access to specific network resources (e-government), enabling both national services (health, voting, social security) and local services depending on municipal needs and requirements (transport, education); 3) *interoperability*: a unique card used throughout the country.

The solution adopted

Document layout

The document is a plastic ID1 format "hybrid" card with, as mentioned above, both a chip and an optical memory band. The dimensions of the card are based on the standard format described in ISO/IEC 7810:1995 for non-embossed identification cards: length 53.92/54.03 mm, width 85.47/85.72 mm, thickness 0.68/0.84 mm.

On the front side of the card, the layout has an upper zone for personal data and a photo of the holder, and a lower zone – ICAO MRZ (Machine Readable Zone) – for the electronic reading of the same data, codified on three lines and printed in OCRB, readable with appropriate devices.

On the back side, besides other personal data, there is a chip, an optical memory band and a security hologram (Figure 1).

Figure 1. **Instruments (solution adopted)**

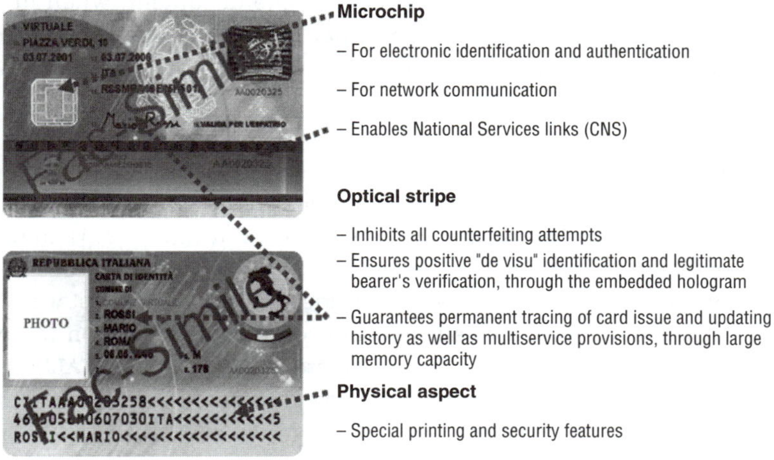

Microchip

– For electronic identification and authentication

– For network communication

– Enables National Services links (CNS)

Optical stripe

– Inhibits all counterfeiting attempts
– Ensures positive "de visu" identification and legitimate bearer's verification, through the embedded hologram
– Guarantees permanent tracing of card issue and updating history as well as multiservice provisions, through large memory capacity

Physical aspect

– Special printing and security features

Print

As to security printing features present on the front side of the card, there is a blue stripe in the separation line between the upper and lower zone.

Visible on this stripe (with suitable enlargement) is a positive microprint with the words "REPUBBLICA ITALIANA".

On the upper right corner of the document is an Optically Variable Ink (OVI) element reproducing the map of Italy. This printed element, made by serigraphy, changes from blue to violet depending on the angle of observation, obtained by tilting or moving the document.

A security background with two variable elements in blue is present.

On the back side of the card is a security background with an image in a scale of grey with a blue graphical element.

Laser engraving

On the front side of the card, the first piece of personalised data is the name of the municipality that issued the document. This element is obtained by laser engraving; it differs from other personalised elements due to the depth of the engraving with respect to the paper surface. The same technique is used to obtain the document numbering, which appears on both the front of the card and the back, in the area below the hologram.

On the back of the document, a positive microprint reproducing the symbol of the Republic of Italy is present: an enlargement of the image will show a positive microprint with the letters "CIE".

A fluorescent invisible print is used on the document: when lit by a UV light, this element will appear evenly dark and the centre of the element will reveal a pink-coloured image representing the globe, with "CIE" in the foreground.

Security hologram

On the back of the document in the upper right corner is a metallised hologram realised by Dot Matrix and 2D/3D mixed techniques. Holding the hologram near a light source (halogen if possible), one can see in the foreground the Italian Republic symbol inside an orbit; both the star and the wheel in the picture have a kinetic effect of contraction-expansion when the card is tilted. In the background, the microtext "REPUBBLICA ITALIANA" is continuously repeated. By rotating the hologram around the horizontal axis, the colours of the image change.

Optical memory band

The zone reserved for memory (reading and writing through optical technology) is on the back of the document and looks like a metallic horizontal stripe. On the upper side of the band, there is a 3 mm stripe on which the symbol of the Italian Republic is continuously repeated between two guilloche elements. On the lower left part of the band is a microprint reproducing the name of the Italian Stationery Office and Government Mint, the producer of the card. On the left part of the optical memory band, there is an embedded hologram – realised in the personalisation phase – reproducing the document number and the photo of the document holder. This feature, like the hologram, is more visible under a specific light source (see Figures 2 and 3).

Figure 2. **Instruments (solution adopted)**

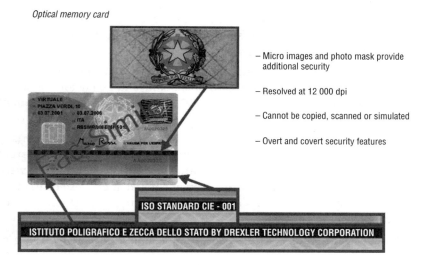

Optical memory card

– Micro images and photo mask provide additional security

– Resolved at 12 000 dpi

– Cannot be copied, scanned or simulated

– Overt and covert security features

ISO STANDARD CIE - 001

ISTITUTO POLIGRAFICO E ZECCA DELLO STATO BY DREXLER TECHNOLOGY CORPORATION

Figure 3. **Instruments (solution adpoted)**

Optical memory card

– Unique capability in card technology
– Memory permanently marked with card holder ID
– W.O.R.M. media cannot be erased or altered
– Up to 16 partitions for different applications
– Maximum safeguarding of privacy
– One reserved partition for ID purposes
– Free partitions for future applications
– Personal information are PIN protected
– It can store any biometric information

The optical memory stripe (LaserCard) is an optical technology medium that can be written and read by a laser beam via the same technologies as the common compact disc (CD-ROM). The material used is polycarbonate, a rugged plastic used in jet-fighter canopies that is one thousand times more resistant than PVC, and it is neither toxic nor as difficult to recycle as PVC. The optical memory itself consists of a thin metallic film obtained by a photolithographic process. Data recording takes place through micro-perforation of the optical substrate by a laser beam. The standards for the optical stripe are: ISO 10373-1/5, ISO 11693, ISO 11694. The advantage of the optical memory stripe is that it provides maximum security against counterfeiting through WORM (Write Once Read Many) technology that allows updating or adding of new information but not the erasing or changing of data.

The stripe's standards of data storage capacity are 2.8 megabytes for the 35 mm type (the one adopted for the US Green Card) and 1.0 MB for the 16 mm type (the one adopted for the Italian EIC and the Canadian Permanent Resident Card).

The stripe thus provides better biometric information storage than any other portable medium, for an absolutely reliable ID check. It can store fingerprints – all ten – not only as an algorithm as happens with microprocessors but the whole image, even encrypted. It can also be used for voice recognition, retina or iris scan, hand geometry, and 2D and 3D face recognition.

The optical memory stripe also offers a maximum safeguarding of privacy.

It makes immediate checks possible between the card and its bearer by means of biometrics, without being linked to any database. The personal data stored in the card's memory are also protected.

The capability of performing off-line ID checks is tremendously advantageous in terms of security, swiftness, and reduction of the whole infrastructure cost.

Recent evolution and prospects

The Italian Home Office, together with the Ministry for Innovation and Technologies and the National Association of Municipalities, has unveiled the IEIC Programme.

The second phase (following the success of the first pilot phase, which involved 83 municipalities issuing 170 000 cards) will see the issuing of 2.8 million IEIC cards in 55 large, medium and small municipalities by the end of 2004. The final objective of the Italian Government is to provide all Italian citizens with the electronic document within five years.

Programme procedures have been designed to guarantee both the issuing authorities and citizens security, privacy, and technology optimisation.

The EIC will, among other functions, serve as the core instrument of the new national electronic polling system which has already had successful tryouts in the cities of Parma and Campobasso.

Last but not least, the municipalities will play an important role in the EIC system, bringing the citizens closer to institutions.

Services provided

The EIC will contain not only personal demographic data and the fiscal code, but also emergency health information, as allowed by law. It may contain other information, *e.g.* that necessary to generate the biometric key or for the digital signature, as well as for electronic polling. It may also enable electronic payments from citizens to the public administration.

Given the high functional versatility and advanced performance of the EIC, a very strict set of security and utilisation rules has been devised and adopted before beginning the second phase. The Italian Government deems it essential that all issues of security, privacy, and equal opportunities between citizens and foreign residents be taken on board into the EIC programme.

The production process

The procedure that Italian citizens have to follow to get their EIC is similar to the one followed at present for the paper identity document, which will keep the process simple and straightforward. Nevertheless, issuance of the EIC requires sophisticated interaction among all levels of government actors – national, regional and municipal – and between them and private players.

As to the production process, there are four main phases in which both private and public actors are involved.

Card production

Actors in the production phase are the microchip manufacturers, laser band manufacturer (LCSistemia/Drexler – see Figures 4 and 5) and IPZS. In this phase, the microchip and laser band manufacturers supply their products to IPZS, which embeds them onto the blank EIC cards and stores them pending the emission request from the municipalities.

- **Drexler Technology Corporation** created optical memory cards in 1981, and currently owns over 50 US patents related to optical data storage.
- Drexler Technology's manufacturing facility in Mountain View, California, has an annual production capacity of up to 25 million cards.

Figure 4. **The actors involved: company profiles**

Istituto Poligrafico e Zecca dello Stato (IPZS – Italian Stationery Office and Government Mint) is entrusted with the printing and distribution of the Official Gazette and other government publications, in traditional as well as technologically advanced formats (online and off-line). IPZS is also involved in the development and production of anti-forgery security systems and products (plastic cards, holograms, paper for office use and for banknotes, saving certificates, stamps, motor vehicle identification plates, computerised cartography), for the Italian public administration and private clients alike.

IPZS is also editor in the fields of art and culture – with a wide range of publications (including reproduction in facsimile of ancient manuscripts) – scientific literature and law publications (quarterly reviews of Italian and European Law), both in traditional and multimedia formats.

Finally, in addition to coining the euro for the domestic market and the Republic of San Marino, IPZS produces and supplies medals, honours, seals, dyes and metallic countersigns for public and private bodies. It also produces coins and banknotes for foreign countries. foreign countries.

Figure 5. **The actors involved: company profiles**

- **Drexler Technology Corporation** created optical memory cards in 1981, and currently owns over 50 US patents related to optical data storage.
- Drexler Technology's manufacturing facility in Mountain View, California, has an annual production capacity of up to 25 million cards.
- **LaserCard Systems Corporation** was founded by Drexler Technology in 1991 to develop, market and sell optical card-based systems.
- **Laser Memory Card S.r.l. of Italy** is since 1994 the most representative partnership.
- **L.C. Sistemia S.p.a.** is the only European manufacturer of the Optical Memory Card reader/writer and Optical Memory cards.

Initialisation phase

In this phase the actors are the municipalities and IPZS. The local government requests the necessary cards from IPZS, which must then:

● Initialise the microchip and laser card structure.

● Install the microchip security access and privilege.

THE SECURITY ECONOMY – ISBN 92-64-10772-X – © OECD 2004

- Generate the ID serial card number.
- Print constant and security elements.
- Embed the hologram in the laser card.
- Submit the emission request to the Italian Home Office and await the order to proceed.

Activation phase

The actors involved in this phase are the Italian Home Office, the municipalities and IPZS.

Once it has received the green light from the Italian Home Office, IPZS traces the ministerial answer in its database, merges the EIC ID number with the local government ID and sends the merged result to the Italian Home Office. Finally, IPZS sends the "white EIC" to the local governments that requested them.

Issuance phase

Here the actors involved are the same as above, plus the citizen who requests the document.

The municipality:

- Gathers the citizen's personal data (photo and other identity information).
- Generates the card's public/private key and the user's PIN.
- Sends an IEIC certificate request in PKCS#10 format (= IEIC ID + IEIC Kpub + encrypted personal data) to the Home Office and waits for the final "Ready to release".
- Inserts the personal data and the IEIC certificate into the microchip and laser card.
- Opens the national services on the chips.
- Installs national directories.
- Opens the local services on the chip's local directories.
- Prints the personal data onto the white IEIC.
- Prints the user's PIN.
- Releases the EIC to the citizen.

Other applications

European driving licence

By 2005, the EU will standardise the driving licence on a new type of plastic card, with individual countries allowed, if they wish, to include a microchip for more information. This is mainly to guard against licence fraud but also to harmonise the rules regarding medical and eye checks for older drivers, and to bring in minimum requirements for the initial qualification and training of driving examiners – thus creating increasing similarities between driving tests throughout the EU.

Permesso di Soggiorno (Immigrant Visa)

Together with the emission of the EIC, the Italian Government counts on issuing the Permesso di Soggiorno Elettronico for non-EU residents living in Italy. The card will be technologically identical to the EIC, with a chip and an optical memory card. It will also offer the same high levels of security. The document will have the citizen's identity information and the Certificate of Authentication that will allow the identification online. The Permesso di Soggiorno Elettronico will allow non-EU residents living in Italy to use the same services provided by the administrations electronically, facilitating the work of the police.

In all, the Italian Government's choice of a hybrid solution for its new ID card promises both unparalleled security and functional versatility.

ISBN 92-64-10772-X
The Security Economy
OECD 2004

Chapter 7

Assessing the Economic Trade-offs of the Security Economy*

by

Tilman Brück
Department of International Economics
German Institute for Economic Research (DIW Berlin)
Germany

* The author is grateful for helpful comments from Reza Lahidji, Patrick Lenain, Barrie Stevens and participants at the OECD Security Economy seminar. Till Stowasser provided excellent research assistance. The usual disclaimer applies.

1. Introduction

The world seems to have become less secure since September 11, 2001. A variety of risks are appearing, are being noticed or are being feared more now than before the deadly attacks on New York and Washington. These risks include the new global terrorism, large-scale electrical blackouts, wars in the Middle East, an increase in computer viruses, worms and spam, attacks by snipers, e-commerce fraud, anthrax attacks, petrol strikes, and international financial instability.

This chapter presents some economic concepts common to the analyses of these "new" sources of insecurity and suggests some policy recommendations for the new security economy. The analysis that follows is based on a broad definition of risk, encompassing social and private risks and public and private goods suitable for reducing them. The chapter addresses the key trade-offs that actors have to resolve and suggests policy instruments for dealing with these trade-offs. It is found that the indirect effects by private agents and by governments outweigh the direct costs of insecurity. However, no single concept of optimal allocation of risks and security exists. Policy makers should choose a portfolio of policy instruments to reduce, deal with and compensate insecurity.

2. Characterising the security economy

What is the security economy?

"Risk" can have several economic meanings. First, risk describes the possibility of an event occurring or being induced. Examples may include the likelihood of a cheque bouncing or of a cheque fraudster being detected. In this chapter, such events typically cause substantial damage.

Second, risk refers to the variance or volatility of economic indicators such as exchange rates or future investment returns. These movements may induce costs to some economic actors.

Third, risk can be defined as an indicator that is close to a threshold. Again, there may be some cost or loss involved in being close to a threshold. This is akin to the concept of vulnerability. An example is the growth rate of the gross domestic product (GDP). If it drops to below 0% growth for one or two periods, then an economy can be said to be in recession, even if it grew strongly in the previous and subsequent periods. An economy growing at a

102

much lower average but always positive rate over all these periods, however, would never have experienced a recession. The costs of a given variation hence depend on the distance to a given threshold.

These forms of risk are inherently private to varying degrees. Therefore the analysis of and the policies for the security economy differ from the analysis of and the policies for national security. The latter is the prototypical public good. Such a good is non-rivalling in consumption: each citizen enjoys the full amount of defence produced, without restricting the consumption of other citizens. Furthermore, it is impossible to exclude citizens from the provision of national security. The distinction between private and public goods will be important in the analysis that follows.

Insecurity is here defined as an aggregated and unquantifiable form of risk. There are different sources of risk and hence of insecurity in the economy. These are related to the forces of nature, globalisation and technological, social, and political developments on the one hand and economic or market forces on the other. The former focus could be seen to be exogenous to economic developments, at least in the short term or as viewed by individual economic agents. Examples may include global warming, increased international migration, technical innovations such as the Internet or wireless communications, and political events such as war and terrorism. The latter forces are endogenous to the process of economic decision making and may be influenced by individual agents to some extent. Examples include stock market fluctuations, inflation and insurance contracts.

This distinction between exogenous and endogenous threats raises two important points. First, the classification of a given risk as exogenous or endogenous may vary depending on the observer, and that has important implications. Second, security policy recommendations will vary depending on which type of threat or risk is under consideration, such as pre-emptive (*ex ante*) *versus* compensatory (*ex post*) policies.

The security economy will here be defined as those activities preventing, dealing with and mitigating insecurity in the economy. That broad definition would include private and public activities in both legal and illegal areas of the economy. Narrower versions of the definition (such as a focus on state spending for homeland security, or private spending for anti-crime devices) may be adopted by other authors for different purposes.

How large is the security economy?

Such a broadly defined security sector is not easily measured using standard economic concepts. One problem is that not all security measures translate into higher costs or spending, thus making the measurement of non-financial aspects very difficult for economists. In addition, double-counting of spending items will occur to a large extent. For example, an anti-theft device built into a car may be considered private security spending or private automotive spending. Most estimates of security spending are either rough guesses of magnitudes and extremely unreliable, or very specific and narrow measures that do not permit an extrapolation of total security spending trends. Most studies of the implications of the security economy are based on assumptions, with the findings reflecting initial assumptions.

Private spending in the security sector could encompass the consumption of and investments in security measures by households and firms (such as alarm systems, safes, surveillance systems and security guards). Broadly speaking, insurance contributions could also be considered as security spending, since they represent a key market response to the existence of risks. Public spending on security could also involve consumption and investment in civilian matters (such as education, prevention and protection programmes) in addition to security-related spending on judiciary, police and military items (e.g. new personnel or equipment in these fields). In addition, legislators can agree new rules governing security (for example in the field of data protection or civil rights) that may have strong economic implications but that cannot be measured directly using financial concepts or categories such as time input (Hobijn, 2002).

Some estimates put the security sector's global annual turnover at over USD 100 billion (see Stevens, in this volume). Much of that spending takes place in the United States. One estimate places US private security spending at USD 40 billion per year (Lenain et al., 2002). Other OECD member countries have significant but smaller security sectors. For example, turnover is thought to be around EUR 4 billion in Germany and EUR 3 billion in both France and the United Kingdom. Historical growth rates for the industry appear to average 7-8% per year worldwide, outpacing economic growth rates by a considerable margin (Stevens). It is not even clear if the security economy is continuing to expand rapidly. One key reason for this ambiguity is that an increase in risks has two opposing impacts on security spending: a substitution effect raising demand for risk reduction and an income effect due to risk-induced general economic downturn, reducing the ability to buy such services.

Public sector spending data are in general more widely available. However, public sector spending on security suffers from the same delineation problem as private spending on security. The available data hence vary significantly. Dietz (2002), for example, calculates that the German Government spent EUR 52.1 billion (or 2.5% of GDP) on security matters in 2000.

3. Effects of the security economy

This section will outline some of the economic effects of insecurity itself, and some of the effects of the responses to insecurity. This distinction is important, as the majority of the costs of insecurity may not stem from the actual risks themselves but from people's and governments' strong reactions to the perception of such risks. The scale of these two effects will also be discussed.

How is the economy affected by insecurity?

Insecurity imposes costs on people who are risk-averse. Most economic agents would prefer a world of less insecurity, or with less risk, and are willing to pay a premium for the reduction of risks. In fact, however, there are three kinds of insecurity costs: the direct costs resulting from the underlying risky *event* itself; the indirect first-order costs induced by the *agent's* reaction to the threat; and finally, the indirect second-order costs that are caused by the *policy* responses to the event and to the agents' reactions.

Direct effects of insecurity include losses in property rights, output, utility, health or lives resulting from events such as theft, fraud, computer viruses, power cuts or terrorism. The first-order negative effects contain the responses by the parties directly affected, such as precautionary information technology (IT) measures taken by a company targeted by computer viruses, or the expenses for re-establishing the initial state prior to the negative event. The second-order indirect effects include the costs of the measures implemented by government in response to actual or perceived risks. These may include economic policies or more general political reactions to threats and insecurity.

A case study emphasising this point is the international financial stability post-9/11. Global capital markets are tightly interlinked. News spreads rapidly, causing spillover, or contagion, effects. Both the great volatility and the potential instability of financial markets create risks for other economic actors. Hence US officials closed financial markets for four trading days after the terrorist attacks of 9/11. However, US and other important capital markets abroad proved to be far more resilient than predicted. Equity prices all over the world fell sharply, but only in the short run. For example, the Dow Jones Index returned to its pre-attack level within 40 trading days.

A recent empirical investigation of the response of capital markets to cataclysmic events concluded that US capital markets have improved their response times in the last fifty years (Chen and Siems, 2004). This may be explained by more efficient banking and financial sectors, providing the necessary liquidity to promote market stability. Also, the fast and well-co-ordinated responses by international monetary authorities helped stabilise the global financial system. Earlier events do not appear to have been more dramatic than recent events; instead, the economy had not been able to deal with crises in an adequate way. This observation emphasises that it is not only the nature of a disastrous incident that determines its consequences, but also the manner in which it is handled.

How is the economy affected by the response to insecurity?

It is the multitude of indirect effects of risks, such as changes in preferences, information, perception, behavioural patterns, incentives, modes of economic organisation and economic and security policy, that dominate the costs of insecurity.

However, these reactions may not always be justified – even if they are voluntary – because the degree of insecurity is a matter of perception. Actual risks are extremely hard to assess. Not only are there few unbiased data available, but there is also much evidence that people, and by extension policy makers, are poor judges of objective levels of risks. Especially when strong emotions such as fear are involved, people tend to focus on worst-case scenarios rather than on the probability of the outcome occurring. As a result, agents overestimate minor risks and neglect significant risks (Sunstein, 2003).

In addition, the public representation of insecurity is very skewed. Airline crashes, for example, receive more column inches in newspapers than fatal car accidents, although the former cause fewer casualties than the latter. For both reasons it is likely that the private sector and policy makers over-provide security measures and legislation, so that the costs of security may easily exceed its benefits.

First-order indirect effects: the agent's reaction

A key issue affecting the nature of the first-order indirect effects is the level of private sector security spending. Such spending may express an underlying desire to protect production or to enhance a firm's products. As such, security spending may be voluntary or a response to market forces. Or, it could be obligatory as a result of new security legislation. This distinction has an impact on the competitiveness of firms.

In the first case, firms decide to spend money on security in the short term to minimise long-term costs (e.g. by spending on building security to avoid or deter fire, thieves or terrorists attacks). Such spending is akin to insurance spending and reflects a firm's information, perception and preferences. Firms can be said to self-insure against certain risks. It is likely that some firms have higher costs than others, e.g. as a result of their location in high-risk zones.

In the second case, firms respond to market forces for enhanced security measures, for example because employees require employers to have such security measures (e.g. protecting expatriate staff on high-risk postings) or because more security has to be embedded into a firm's products (e.g. alarm systems in cars). In these cases, costs rise but potentially revenues rise as well, or are prevented from falling. Such measures may involve many firms in a market, although some firms may opt to provide lower security and hence lower-quality products and thus occupy a different niche of the market. An intermediate level of cost differentiation may thus obtain.

In the third case, firms are legally obliged to implement certain security measures (e.g. airlines serving the United States). In this case, the extra security spending acts like an environmental regulation by pushing costs but not raising private benefits to the firm. Instead, such regulation is imposed to raise social welfare, but its costs are borne only by the firms in the first instance. Within-sector productivity will fall as a result of such enforced spending. In parallel, new sectors may emerge to service the new security needs, as can be observed in the environmental service sector. For a closed economy, this then implies that costs are borne uniformly by all firms in a given sector. Internationally, this may not hold and raises important trade policy issues.

The third case also contrasts with a new tax imposed on a sector. Taxes also reduce productivity and may affect certain firms uniformly. However, taxes have the important implication of raising tax revenue, which can then be used to achieve some other social good or to compensate some other actor. Also, in the case of taxation, the taxable sector and the sector at risk may differ, while in the case of state security spending the two are necessarily the same. Hence in the latter case, threatened sectors may be doubly affected by the new insecurity, through both the security risk and the security legalisation. Depending on circumstances, this raises the policy recommendation to diverge security measures and their financing to reduce the burden of new security measures.

In order to illustrate how severely the economy can be influenced by first-order indirect effects, it is useful to consider possible impacts.

Greater insecurity (e.g. due to terrorist attacks) may lead to the redesign of supply chains which in turn reduces the benefits from just-in-time production processes. Alternatively, firms may prefer to source their inputs from local suppliers if these are less affected by certain insecurities. Such local suppliers may be more reliable, but also more expensive. In the long term, such cost pressures may induce a variety of changes, such as increases in inventories, investments in new technologies and changes in the balance of horizontal or vertical integration (Sheffi, 2001; Hodges and McFarlane, in this volume).

Other indirect effects of higher insecurity include higher transaction costs of conducting business, including higher transport costs and higher transport insurance rates. This will reduce trade flows in the transport and tourism sectors, both domestically and internationally. The decline in trade could reduce the spread of economic activity and boost geographic clustering. But the more clustered an economy is, the more valuable the clustered target is for terrorists for instance, thus further raising insecurity.

In fact, large-scale violence impacts cities in three ways. First, the safe-harbour effect encourages people to group together so as to have an advantage in defending themselves from attackers, making cities more appealing in times of rising violence. Second, the target effect implies that cities are more attractive targets for violence, which creates an incentive to disperse. Third, the transportation effect suggests that as terrorism often targets means of transportation, violence can increase the effective cost of transportation, which will usually increase the demand for density. However, empirical evidence on war and cities in the 20th century suggests that the effect of wars or terrorism on urbanity is not significant. Having said that, there are notable exceptions – especially in extreme cases like cities in times of war (Glaeser and Shapiro, 2001).

Generally, if insecurity thrives on openness, then firms and households will scale back on openness. For example, less online trade will be conducted in the presence of online fraud, and less international outsourcing will be undertaken in the presence of regular riots, roadblocks or strikes abroad. Change in relative prices as a result of insecurity will lead to a suboptimal reallocation of resources. Therefore, the insecure economy will have lower GDP growth than would obtain otherwise (Lenain *et al.*, 2002).

Higher levels of risk also undermine investors' confidence, reducing their willingness to commit to new projects. Over time, higher risk premiums increase required rates of return on investments, reducing equity prices and biasing investment decisions against high-risk, high-return, long-term investments towards low-risk, low-return, short-term investments. The cumulative effect of such portfolio adjustments is to change the composition of the portfolio, to reduce overall investment and to retard further economic growth. However, markets will also induce positive feedback effects causing structural shifts. These will occur in favour of products and services which have embedded security as an important characteristic (Brück, 2004).

Second-order indirect effects: policy reaction

The US Prohibition Act against alcohol from 1920 to 1933 may serve as an example of how well-meaning state intervention can perversely reduce social welfare. Empirically, it is difficult to estimate if government security regulation itself generally causes further insecurity. Theoretically, this may happen on two levels. First, there may be an element of regulatory insecurity where an increasing density of regulation, though aimed at raising social welfare, increases uncertainty for firms operating in an environment of rising legal obligations. Second, certain types of regulations may trigger illegal responses raising insecurity. For example, the US "War Against Terror" and the "Bush Doctrine" may raise correlated risks, namely the probability of terrorist attacks against American targets abroad. This point also raises the question of whether government action can change the preferences of the private sector, including those of the illegal actors. This point will be examined below in more detail.

The degree of government security regulation is quite large in many economic sectors. For example, more severe inspections and other security regulations create delays at borders, increase shipping times and reduce border permeability, thus reducing trade flows. Such regulation thus exacerbates the effects of insecurity on trade, as outlined above. In addition, standard government regulations in the fields of national defence, crime-fighting and civil rights will impose further costs on businesses (Hobijn, 2002; Philips, 2001; World Bank, 2003). The additional security regulations imply shifting economic resources from the private to the public sector, which will reduce the efficiency-enhancing market powers and also growth.

The aviation sector, for instance, was hit severely by security-related regulation in the wake of 9/11 (Lenain et al., 2002). Higher costs could not be passed on to customers as the degree of competition in the industry was already too high and as terrorist attacks were already causing a negative demand shock. Aviation stock prices also fell, turning what were defensive shares into aggressive shares. Capacity was cut and employment in the sector was markedly reduced. The ongoing structural adjustment process in the aviation industry was thus accelerated by the new insecurity.

The expansion of the public budget itself is also said to have a retarding impact on long-term growth. This is especially true if the defence and the newly founded homeland security budgets are considered.

How large are the effects?

The scales of the effects of insecurity and of the private and public responses to insecurity are difficult to estimate, as was argued above for the size of the security economy. A further complication arises from the nature of insecurity. This is difficult to measure except in the cases of terrorism or war. Many studies proceed by assuming an increase in costs induced by insecurity and then estimate the subsequent changes in trade or growth. Subsequently, the estimates for such effects vary. They can only provide broad indications of the scale and the magnitude of likely effects.

For example, a one-day delay in border controls has been estimated to generate costs of 0.5% of the value of the good (Hummels, 2001). Another calculation suggests rising trading costs of 1-3% *ad valorem* after September 11 (Leonard, 2001). Based on such values, it has been estimated that an increase in US inventories of 10% and an increase in US commercial insurance premiums of 20% would cost 0.1% and 0.3% of GDP per year, respectively (Raby, 2003). Another study calculates an elasticity of trade flows (in volume terms) with respect to transport costs (ad valorem) to lie in the range of –2 to –3.5 (Limao and Venables, 2001).

In international trade the total global welfare losses from 9/11 are relatively low, about USD 75 billion per year (Walkenhorst and Dihel, 2004). Yet some regions and sectors are hit particularly hard. Goods with a low ratio of value to weight (such as agricultural products, textiles, non-metallic minerals and machinery) are vulnerable to an increase in transaction costs. The regions most affected by 9/11 in absolute terms are western Europe, North America and northern Asia. However, southern Asia, North Africa and the Middle East suffer the most damage in relation to the size of their economies, not least due to the higher import dependence. That means that developing countries are particularly affected by the first- and second-order effects of 9/11.

A different methodological approach involves directly estimating the effect of the existence of insecurity on growth of international trade. One such study employing this approach finds that international trade flows are significantly reduced by the existence of terrorism in a trading partner's country (Nitsch and Schumacher, 2004). In the short term, this effect reduced international trade by 4% if the number of terrorist incidents in one country is doubled.

These studies raise a question: to what extent will the negative effects of insecurity wear off in the long term? Increases in efficiency may be obtained by better regulation and implementation (Sheffi, 2001; Hobijn, 2002; Lenain et al., 2002; Walkenhorst and Dihel, 2004; Raby, 2003; World Bank, 2003). Regulation applied may be more targeted, thus reducing unnecessary security measures. Markets may respond to existing measures, finding new ways to communicate, arrange production and deliver goods. Security measures may be successful in deterring or identifying criminals, thus reducing the exposure to risks and hence making the measures superfluous in the long term. This *may* be true. It is, however, not clear if these developments will actually occur. A key policy focus should thus be the monitoring of the security situation, the security policies and their effects on the economy, to adjust measures over time as appropriate.

Poirson (1998) models the impact of security on private investment and growth in 53 developing countries from 1984 to 1995, indicating that increased economic security boosted economic growth by 0.5% to 1.25% per year.

Another analysis cited in Raby (2003) estimates the fall in US investment due to ongoing terrorism threats to be about 0.2% of GDP, the drop being transmitted to other economies through lower US demand for imports.

In assessing the economic effects of security spending, Hobijn claims that neither private nor public spending on security will have a major impact on the economy (2002). Private security spending in the United States will in his view reduce labour productivity by 1.12% and multifactor productivity by 0.65%, which in turn results in only small reductions of American GDP. In addition, he predicts that security-related R&D will not significantly crowd out productivity-enhancing R&D. In regard to public security spending, he calculates that homeland security spending will reduce output only by 0.6% over a five-year period. Judging by the much larger scale of military spending in the 1980s, he believes that to be negligible and to have no effect on the US budget deficit.

However, one should interpret Hobijn's optimistic results with a degree of caution. The analysis contains some important assumptions such that private expenditures for security will only double in the future. Hobijn may also underestimate future public spending by the Bush administration, especially when adding homeland and national security spending in the light of the Iraq war and occupation.

Nordhaus in particular (2002) contradicts Hobijn's line of argument. He cautions not to depend too strongly on governmental estimates of future security budgets. In his view, the costs of wars, for example, are always grossly underestimated, which is perfectly rational from the point of view of the warring government.

Another analysis partly backing Hobijn's view is a simulation of the combined growth effects of increased private expenditures for security (up 0.5% of GDP) and increased military spending (up 1% of GDP) financed through borrowing (Lenain et al., 2002). The study suggests that real GDP would be reduced by about 0.7% after five years. The effect is small but permanent and derives from the consequences of undermining fiscal consolidation. The post-cold war peace dividend is not threatened by such an increase in security-related spending.

4. Aiming for optimal security

This section will discuss the concept of an optimal security policy. It will emphasise the role of preferences in determining an "optimal" outcome, outline the costs and benefits of security policies, and explain some particular aspects of international security policy, especially in the presence of public goods. It will also consider some trade-offs that may be involved in providing security, especially in regard to efficiency, equity and liberty.

Is there an optimal level of security?

The role of preferences

Introducing the concept of optimality in regard to security spending and regulation implies a judgement about preferences and hence the likely nature of benefits from security spending. There are two interpretations of how new information about risks affects preferences. One can either consider the utility function of an individual changing due to new information, or think of new information as revealing previously hidden parts of the preference map of an individual. No matter which of these two interpretations is deemed more likely, preferences affect how insecurity transmits to individuals.

In addition, preferences are a function of perceptions, which increases the complexity of the optimality analysis. Perceptions, being subjective, may not necessarily reflect actual, objective conditions. Hence preferences do not have to reflect a rational response to a changed environment.

On the one hand, preferences can induce a strong wish for security measures if risks are overestimated by agents. In this case the level of security demanded is higher than the social optimum, even though individual utility was maximised.

On the other hand, original preferences may have been reflecting an incorrect assessment of true risks. For example, the events of 9/11 may have revealed to the general public the state of insecurity they are actually facing. This view is supported by evidence that while the likelihood of terrorist attacks has not increased after 9/11, agents assess this risk more realistically (Sandler, 2003). This interpretation also implies that structural changes in the economy (*e.g.* increasing the share of security-related spending) are not inefficient but rather are taking the economy closer to its optimum.

The role of costs and benefits

Investing in security may bring benefits in the long term but creates costs in the short term. The optimal level of security spending occurs where the marginal costs equal the marginal benefits. Hence it is important to uncover the shape of the cost and the benefit functions, at both the private and the social levels.

The costs of security are determined both objectively through a production function with embedded technology, and subjectively through the perception of insecurity. In addition, society may have strong preferences about the difference between type I and type II errors in establishing security. In fact, in the security society, the importance of balancing type I errors (where the innocent goes to jail) and type II errors (where the guilty walks free) may be reversed. Many societies, when protecting their own citizens from attack, prefer to punish the innocent rather than to let the guilty escape having committed atrocities. The opportunity cost of inaction weighs particularly heavily in the security economy. This may hence lead to an otherwise excessive level of security regulation and spending.

The benefits of security to individuals and to society are harder to determine. They include the prevention of direct effects (such as loss of lives, health and physical endowments) and of indirect effects as well as the inherent benefits of security for risk-averse agents.

Private versus social efficiency

National security, like a lighthouse, is a typical public good. Hence, the level of security provided by the private sector will be suboptimal from society's point of view. This is one justification for the public provision or the public regulation of security in a closed economy.

In the international context, competition concerning both the supply of security between countries and the nature of the provision of security could evolve. Some countries may specialise in utilising their comparative advantage in producing secure or insecure goods (such as the respective examples of the United States and Taliban-led Afghanistan in the case of terrorism or Switzerland and some small island states in the case of more or less prudent banking facilities).

In addition, countries may choose different models of providing a given standard of security with an international organisation. NATO, for example, has contained in its history both democracies and dictatorships as well as professional armies and armies of recruits. For companies, there is geographic choice in their production decisions, both in regard to the desired level of security and the nature in which this level is achieved. As a result each country i would then obtain its (individually) optimal level of security s_i^*.

Another problem, however, arises if security is considered to be a weakest-link public good (Hirshleifer, 1983). The prototypical weakest-link public good is a dyke that prevents the rising sea level from flooding an island. Each inhabitant can construct a section of the island's dyke as protection from floods. However, the actual protection equals the height of the lowest section of the dyke. The same concept holds for the general case of international security issues: even if country i spent a lot on security (i.e. it achieved a high s_i^*) it may be negatively affected by another country j with a lower s_j^*: through international trade, country j may export insecurity unwittingly, for example by transporting harmful goods as part of cargo.

At the same time, countries falling behind the evolving international security standards are unable to reap the benefits of globalisation if their territory is no longer seen as being safe or reputable (e.g. guaranteeing security, providing smart technologies and protecting supply chains). Those economies will face higher risk premiums and the cost of protecting assets will rise, reducing foreign direct investments.

It is especially the weakest-link public good nature that emphasises the need for international co-operation and intervention. Whenever the overall level of protection is set by the least contributor, competition fails to achieve the socially optimal level of security. International alliances (such as NATO), organisations (such as the UN) and other agreements, standards and arrangements for mutual control and assistance (such as the IMF) hence are intended to reduce international insecurity by setting minimum standards in the areas of defence, politics and economics. These institutions overcome both the standard and the weakest-link aspects of security as a public good.

This discussion uncovers the complexity of the optimality concept. One cannot identify *the* optimal level of security since there is the need to differentiate the role of objective values from that of subjective preferences, the costs from the benefits of security, the private from the social gains and losses, and the direct from the indirect consequences. Given these intricacies, it is not clear that an absolute or even a local optimum level of security exists.

What are the trade-offs?

As discussed at the beginning of this section, the search for optimal security must necessarily balance the benefits and the costs. Costs in addition to those mentioned signal a number of trades-off between higher security and other goals. In considering the implications of the security economy, five key trade-offs emerge.

Security spending versus other spending

The first trade-off refers to the different types of expenditure by both the private sector and governments, as is common in a war economy. The idea is simple: what is spent on security cannot be spent on consumption or growth-enhancing investments – the butter and guns trade-off mentioned earlier.

The character of *public* spending on military services mainly has to do with consumption; only a small part of military budgets is devoted to research and development (R&D). An economic benefit of military spending is the prevalence of peace. Yet this effect is difficult to estimate in practice. In addition, demand effects will increase GDP growth in the short term but in the long term negative effects may prevail: a large defence budget crowds out public investments, thus lowering total factor productivity. Military spending may also increase the budget deficit, the national debt and (hence) interest rates. Cutting military budgets (or realising a peace dividend) may thus boost growth through higher capital accumulation, a higher civilian labour force and more productive capital allocation for a given security threat. Given the difficulty in controlling for an exogenous security threat and in measuring these effects exactly, the empirical estimates of the growth effects of the peace dividend remain ambiguous (Lenain et al., 2002).

A similar line of reasoning also holds for the case of *private* spending on security. Since output is not positively affected by this spending (especially when spending concerns hiring more guard labour), productivity falls. In addition, productive investments are likely to be crowded out and hence growth is retarded.

Security versus *efficiency*

The second trade-off concerns efficiency. Society achieves efficiency when it gets the greatest amount of utility from available resources or technology. As argued above, aiming for security yields both benefits and costs. Such costs may also include frictions preventing the economy from functioning efficiently.

Efficiency can be visualised as minimal levels of transaction costs, for example when crossing borders or generally in trade. Here there appears to be an obvious trade-off between security and efficiency as more border controls increase security but also reduce the speed and ease with which goods and people are moved. In the long run, however, this trade-off may disappear, as argued above. Security-driven improvements may even facilitate trade in the long run. Additional investments in secure facilities and modern technologies can reduce transaction costs. Security cost pressures could potentially induce reforms in trade-related institutions and infrastructure, with beneficial effects on trade and growth. Better trade facilitation due to deregulation of trade-related sectors, harmonisation of customs services and co-ordination across countries would increase trade among 75 countries by USD 377 billion (World Bank, 2003).

Another example concerns the public versus private provision or regulation of security services and rules. For instance, the United States increased the public sector employment of airport security personnel post-9/11. It is not clear *ex ante* if such services must necessarily be provided by the federal or state government or if, with suitable regulation, private firms may not have provided security more efficiently.

Security versus *globalisation and technological change*

Security's third trade-off may involve globalisation and technological change. It is not clear *ex ante* whether globalisation is compounding or extenuating the problems associated with the security economy. One can identify a race between two effects of globalisation.

On the one hand, the same forces that can bring some countries and sectors such prosperity are highly vulnerable to security threats. Both openness and interdependence enable various risks to destabilise the international economy (Stevens, in this volume). On the other hand, co-ordination, integration and harmonisation that usually go with globalisation may also reduce the scope for insecurity in some areas and make the tracking of the sources of insecurity much easier.

In addition, globalisation is a process that provides ongoing flows of benefits while many forms of insecurity cause one-off, shock-like costs (unlike the fight against insecurity, which may cause ongoing costs too). In an integrated, globalised world economy, building coalitions to fight insecurity by providing public goods may hence be much easier than in a world economy dominated by import-substituting nation states.

Accordingly, Chen and Siems conclude that the globalised world has become more stable in the face of threats (2004). The policy response to 9/11 showed how effectively co-operation can indeed be conducted. International integration made it both possible and necessary for authorities all over the world to share relevant information and to reconcile policies in order to absorb such a tremendous shock.

Globalisation and technological change induce structural change in open economies. The security economy in particular may witness an accelerated structural change (Sheffi, 2001; World Bank, 2003). This may be obtained through technological advances induced by investments in security infrastructure, for example through the automation, surveillance and informational exchange in harbours, airports and border crossings. Globalisation may thus serve as the very means that makes the trade-off between security and efficiency diminish in the long run.

One important policy challenge is the integration of technical security protocols into international organisations, agreements and technical standards (such as the EU, the World Trade Organisation and the International Organization for Standardization). Transparency and harmonisation should be sought to reduce transaction costs. In addition, security concerns should not permit the establishment of non-tariff trade barriers. Another policy implication addresses the role of economic winners and losers from structural change induced by new security regulations. This will be discussed further below.

Security versus equity

The fourth trade-off is both politically and socially sensitive as it concerns the distributional costs of increased security. Analytically, it is not clear ex ante which groups should gain or lose most from higher security. Many security services are provided by the low skilled (such as guards), but many technology-intensive products will be developed by the highly skilled. If international trade is reduced by higher transaction costs, then this may damage employment in those sectors or countries most affected by such measures. Public sector employment may rise if public security spending focuses on judicial, police, customs and military personnel. However, some of their services can also be subcontracted to private providers, which is an important policy option when considering the efficient provision of security, as argued above.

Governments could consider compensating the losers of security measures within their countries. Internationally, this may be particularly important if losers of the security economy (say groups or entire countries losing from reduced trade in developing countries) may themselves be the source of future insecurity. Hence the compensation of losers (and perhaps the taxation of the winners) is strongly related to the causes and the nature of the insecurity. One option may be the accelerated and unilateral reduction of trade barriers for developing countries particularly damaged by the war against terrorism.

Another equity issue is related to the access to security services and products. Lower income groups may, as a result of market forces or due to administrative processes, be excluded from secure products or services. One can also think of social clustering, since indigent groups may only be able to afford property in less safe environments or regions. Policy makers may wish to consider how they can grant egalitarian access to and participation in the security economy.

Security versus *freedom and privacy*

The fifth trade-off also concerns the political decision about the balance of civil rights, privacy and individual freedom versus the possible need to curtail these rights in the pursuit of more security. Internet, computing, mobile and wireless technologies are highly vulnerable to security attacks. At the same time, these technologies can be used to monitor movements, usage and profiles of individuals or goods – both those of consumers and those of potential perpetrators of crimes.

This topic raises a number of interesting and relevant points which, admittedly, are not all or not exclusively the domain of economic analysis. First, there is a clear trade-off between economic freedom and economic growth, at least in the extreme. The empirical estimation of this trade-off may lead to ambiguous results but analytically it should be clear that a high level of regulation and restriction hampers productivity growth and utility maximisation (Paldam and Würtz, 2003).

Second, the evolution of the network economy and the evolution of the security economy are closely related. The opportunity to process and link data of low marginal value is growing dramatically. With it rises both the vulnerability of interconnected and interdependent data systems and the opportunities for tracing criminals. Protecting these systems, using their opportunities and maintaining civil liberties require a fine balancing act. The greater demand for security-induced surveillance and the technological advances in this field facilitate the potential abuse of data mining, social sorting and losses in privacy (Lyon, in this volume).

In fact, many economic sectors require increasingly complex information chains in production. Monitoring – of the origins of food, of industrial chemicals (especially in the European Union), of dangerous waste products – increasingly requires source-to-use chains of information. The use of smart tags can thus be expected to rise dramatically, as will the use of positioning and navigation systems in combination with mobile technology (Hodges and McFarlane, in this volume). These technological and legal developments demonstrate the rising challenges for the security economy and its policy makers. Resolving civil rights and technological security issues should occur in parallel to the implementation of such information chains. Forcing the resolution of security concerns may actually accelerate the development of source-to-use information systems.

5. Policy implications

This section will consider different types of security policies, the rationale for government intervention, and the regulation and organisation of economic security policies.

The main argument to justify government intervention is the public-good nature of security. Agents do not take into account the positive externality their investment in security has on others. As a result, the actual level of security is socially sub-optimal. This is an instance of the prisoner's dilemma.

Such undesired outcomes can be impeded by regulation (forbidding dominating but inefficient strategies or influencing incentives by changing payoffs through subsidies or taxes) or by co-ordination coupled with credible enforcement rules. Clearly there is a need for the state to provide public goods such as security. Yet the thorny question is to what extent the state should be involved and which policy fields deserve priority.

What types of security policies exist?

Security policies can be categorised in various dimensions. First, a threat may be exogenous (such as a natural disaster or a war under some circumstances) or it may be endogenous (such as stock market volatility or insolvency). However, the distinction between exogenous and endogenous risks is not clear-cut. In practice, risks tend to be more exogenous in the short term and at an individual level, and more endogenous in the long term and at a collective level. People may choose to live on a volcano as property prices drop with altitude on volcanoes. Terrorism or war may be targeted, rightly or wrongly, against certain actors in retaliation for their past actions. And insolvencies tend to occur after past management errors.

Second, policies aimed at reducing our exposure to risks can act *ex ante* (for example by installing anti-virus software) or *ex post*, which refers mainly to punitive (for example by punishing hackers) or compensatory action. The *ex ante* actions can be differentiated more subtly into the actions of prevention, deterrence, pre-emption and protection. Some of these policies may not be security policies in a narrow sense. Yet it is a useful reminder that reducing economic insecurity involves many more policy fields than law and order or economics.

In the international context, pre-emption and protection have different externalities (Sandler, 2003; Trajtenberg, 2003). While pre-emption carried out by an individual state reduces the overall probability that, say, a terrorist attack will occur (a positive externality), the strategy to protect an individual target just reduces the probability that this specific target will be hit while raising the probability for other targets (a negative externality). The first case leads to a global under-investment in pre-emption activities while the latter implicates a global over-investment in defensive spending. Both externalities justify governmental intervention through the provision of security, regulation and international co-operation.

Third, combining these two dimensions generally suggests that for exogenous risks *ex post* policies may be more appropriate while for endogenous risks *ex ante* policies appear most effective. The probability of an exogenous event can be swayed neither by *ex ante* policies nor by *ex post* policies. The costs that such an event entails, however, can be reduced with a compensating *ex post* policy. In the case of endogenous risks a good policy attempts to reduce the risk for the malevolent event to occur. These policies have by definition an *ex ante* character. One can also construct counter-examples: the announcement of an *ex post* policy has also *ex ante* implications, since people anticipate these interventions. Compensatory schemes, for instance, are considered a major factor determining how much people expose themselves to risks.

Fourth, public policies can best provide those aspects of security that are a public good, such as national security. The private sector, on the other hand, has an important role to play in choosing its exposure to private risks. Here regulation and general standards are a more important role for public policy, not the detailed provision of secure goods and services that can also be provided by market forces.

Fifth, security policies can defend against a risk more or less aggressively. In the case of an endogenous risk, there is the danger that either approach may induce a change in the risk. For example, guarding American embassies more heavily abroad after the dual attacks on US embassies in Kenya and Tanzania in the 1990s reduced embassy bombings but led to an increase in shootings and abductions of embassy personnel away from the embassies themselves (Sandler and Enders, 2004).

Sixth, in addition to the direct security policies, further policies may aim to reduce the costs of insecurity. This may serve the purpose of reducing the impact of insecurity but also of making deliberate acts of insecurity less attractive to the perpetrators. Frey and Luechinger, for example, suggest that raising the marginal costs of terrorists to undertake terrorist attacks by adopting deterrence policies may not be the best response to such threats (2004). Instead, terrorism may be fended off more effectively by abating the expected benefits of terrorist acts for the prospective terrorists. Such a policy could be based on strengthening decentralised decision making, since a strike against authority would then have only little effect on the stability of the polity and the economy as a whole.

Finally, the analysis of security policies should differentiate policy instruments. Information and institutions are one group of policies to achieve deterrence and punishment. Since the probability of malevolence tends to be overestimated by individuals, information should be used to make risks more transparent. One policy instrument is regulation, supervision and co-ordination, while another is the provision of financial incentives and disincentives, for example through fiscal policy. For instance, in addition to the under-provision of security, a market economy may also under-invest in R&D. As R&D generates spillovers for society, the social rate of return is typically higher than the private rate, and hence private investment in R&D typically falls short of the socially desirable level. Hence, even if security were a private good, there would be a case for state subsidies for security-related R&D.

The public debate over fighting terrorism since 9/11, for instance, has focused quite strongly on security spending and the adjustment of civil rights while neglecting some other instruments such as international co-ordination, political signals or even, at times, deliberate disinterest. Most importantly, the public debate often has disregarded the question of how the market may help solve some of the problems that society faces, instead focusing strongly on government intervention, regulation and spending.

How to regulate the security economy?

Even if government regulation of the security economy is necessary, it should be tailored with care. Incentives, expectations and market powers should be emphasised to raise the efficiency of the intervention. Crowding out should be avoided to reduce the negative secondary effects of intervention. Public-private co-operation may be feasible in more cases than previously envisaged, for example in providing security services or in implementing new regulatory schemes (Sheffi, 2001). At the same time, compensatory or complementary liberalising policies are important to provide ongoing growth stimuli and to generate the surplus to assist vulnerable groups in the global security economy. This applies especially in the area of transport costs and world trade, where additional trade access may be provided to countries that risk losing out in the security economy (Leibfritz, 2003; World Bank, 2003).

In addition to these co-ordination mechanisms, the market also provides some mechanisms to enhance voluntary security spending. For example, agents investing in security may pay lower premiums in insurance contracts. Such outcomes can be enhanced further by regulation defining liability, which increases the incentives of the guilty party to act responsibly.

The post-9/11 insurance sector is in fact an example of the importance of regulation versus subsidy and of the potential role of market forces in alleviating the economic costs of insecurity. Insurance firms exist to deal with insecurity. However, even the world's largest reinsurers faced fundamental problems after the attacks of 9/11 (Wolgast and Ruprecht, 2003). Again, the direct effects of the terrorist attacks are not the heart of the problem. It is true that with damages of about USD 30-58 billion, 9/11 represents the largest insurance event in history (Lenain et al., 2002) This impact was, however, not strong enough to cause any major bankruptcies among insurance companies.

Indirect effects are responsible for making the insurance sector the focus of economic scrutiny: large-scale terrorist attacks are perceived to be more likely since 9/11. Insurance companies increased the maximal damage considered probable in their calculations, letting premiums rise by up to 30% (Lenain et al., 2002). Even more momentous is the fact that coverage was either significantly reduced or contracts including insurance against terrorist attacks were entirely cancelled. As a result, major terrorist attacks were no longer fully insurable, which is a problem since the willingness to bear risks is a scarce factor of production: in a world of greater uncertainty fewer investments will take place, thus reducing long-term growth. In particular, investments in innovative and venturesome but specifically growth-enhancing projects are omitted.

One can already foresee what the indirect second-order effects are to be about. There are audible calls for the government to act. Since the private sector turns out to be unable to insure terrorism-related risks, the state should back the system through subsidies and guarantees. While an intervention in itself may be favourable, the regulatory scheme must be carefully designed. Matters of incentive compatibility in particular bear the risk that the government may even exacerbate the adverse effects of insecurity. In fact, after September 2001 the insurance sector was helped not by direct payments but by re-regulation of the reinsurance business in cases of large terrorist attacks. Germany, as the United Kingdom before it, set up a state-backed but privately organised and limited "re-reinsurer" for terrorist claims. Importantly, this scheme reinforced the incentives of the private sector to guard against terrorist risks and helped the market price the value of anti-terrorist insurance.

The government does not, however, stand alone in responding to the changed environment. Private sector initiatives and public-private partnerships are emerging, specifically tailored to cover major damage risks. German Extremus AG may serve as an example for how multi-pillar risk-sharing mechanisms involving insurers, reinsurers, pooling structures and governments as an insurer of last resort may offer a valid alternative. Extremus AG, founded by 16 major insurance companies, offers polices exclusively tailored for major damage risks (more than EUR 25 million). The company's capacity is EUR 13 billion, consisting of three coverage layers. The German Government only provides a guarantee for the third layer, which is solely drawn on if the first two layers are depleted (Lenain *et al.*, 2002; Wolgast and Ruprecht, 2003).

Another way a market economy could deal with insuring terrorism-induced risks is through so-called catastrophe bonds, which are associated with both high returns and high risks. While trading the risks on the capital market seems an efficient solution to the problem in theory, in practice it has not really worked so far (Leibfritz, 2003; Lenain *et al.*, 2002).

How should security policy be co-ordinated?

The prisoner's dilemma can be solved through regulation, as argued above, or through co-ordination. This is particularly applicable in instances where security is dependent on the weakest link, as argued in Section 4.

These problems are similar to network externalities where a community will adopt a standard from among several competing standards after enough members have adopted this standard. In the security economy, the incentive for any agent to invest in security is an increasing function of how many others have already done so.

Co-ordination can be enhanced through sharing information, repeated contacts, developing reputation, agreeing (even informally) sanction mechanisms, and sharing technical standards. International organisations such as the International Air Transport Association (IATA) for the airline industry can stipulate rules and regulations for member states. A key policy issue relates to the sanctions that are implemented locally within member states, which apply in the case of locally deviant behaviour.

Generally, governments should refrain from executing extreme policies. Competition alone cannot solve the problems. Neither can state intervention. The best results may be achieved by a portfolio of policies combining political, economic, legal and social means. This policy mix must be sought to achieve a reasonably high global security standard. Institutions such as the OECD should play a vital role in this co-ordination game.

6. Conclusions

The recent rise of global terrorism has focused the attention of policy makers worldwide on the emergence, effects and regulations of the security economy. The term "security economy" has no strict economic meaning, encompassing as it does many different activities in the private and public sectors. In addition, there is no unique optimal level of security. However, this chapter demonstrated that insecurity has significant direct effects and even more important indirect first- and second-order effects. These encompass the behavioural responses by agents and the subsequent policy responses by governments, respectively.

Policy interventions need to be carefully thought out, considering agents' preferences and perceptions, the costs and benefits of actions, and the international dimension of insecurity. The private sector has an important role to play in ensuring the efficient provision of private security. Domestic aspects of security may be better provided by governments while international security must be achieved through global co-operation. Governmental intervention in markets and an increased private provision of security may raise security, but this may come at the expense of efficiency, equity or freedom. Only a portfolio of government policies can address the multiple dimensions of security.

Bibliography

ARCE, D.G. and T. SANDLER (2001), "Transnational Public Goods: Strategies and Institutions", *European Journal of Political Economy*, 17(3), pp. 493-516.

BRÜCK, T. (2004), "The Economic Consequences of Terror: Guest Editor's Introduction", *European Journal of Political Economy*, forthcoming.

BRÜCK, T. and S. SCHUBERT (2003), "Krieg und Wiederaufbau im Irak", *DIW Wochenbericht*, 70(18), pp. 291-297.

CHEN, A.H. and T.F. SIEMS (2004), "The Effects of Terrorism on Global Capital Markets", *European Journal of Political Economy*, forthcoming.

DIETZ, O. (2002), "Öffentliche Ausgaben für äußere und innere Sicherheit", *Wirtschaft und Statistik*, 4, pp. 310-315.

FREY, B.S. and S. LUECHINGER (2004), "Decentralization as a Disincentive for Terror", *European Journal of Political Economy*, forthcoming.

GLAESER, E.L. and J. M. SHAPIRO (2001), "Cities and Warfare: The Impact of Terrorism on Urban Form", *NBER Working Paper Series* 8696.

HIRSHLEIFER, J. (1983), "From Weakest-Link to Best-Shot: The Voluntary Provision of Public Goods", *Public Choice* 41, pp. 371-386.

HOBIJN, B. (2002), "What Will Homeland Security Cost?", *Economic Policy Review*, 8(2), pp. 21-33.

HODGES, S. and D. MCFARLANE (2004), "RFID: The Concept and the Impact", in this volume and presented at the OECD Forum for the Future on "The Security Economy: What Trade-Offs in an Open and Mobile Society?", Paris, 8 December 2003.

HUMMELS, D. (2001), "Time As a Trade Barrier", Mimeo, Department of Economics, Purdue University, West Lafayette/Indiana.

KUNREUTHER, H. and G. HEAL (2003), "Interdependent Security", *The Journal of Risk and Uncertainty*, 26(2/3), pp. 231-249.

LEIBFRITZ, W. (2003), "Auswirkungen des Terrorismus auf die Volkswirtschaften und Implikationen für die Wirtschaftspolitik", *Ifo Schnelldienst*, 56(1), pp. 14-20.

LENAIN, P., M. BONTURI and V. KOEN (2002), "The Economic Consequences of Terrorism", *OECD Economics Department Working Papers*, 334.

LEONARD, J.S. (2001), "Impact of the September 11, 2001 Terrorist Attacks on North American Trade Flows", Manufacturers Alliance E-Alert, Arlington, Virginia.

LIMAO, N. and A.J. VENABLES (2001), "Infrastructure, Geographical Disadvantage, Transport Costs and Trade", *World Bank Economic Review*, 15, pp. 451-479.

LYON, D. (2004), "Surveillance Technologies: Trends and Social Implications", in this volume and presented at the OECD Forum for the Future on "The Security Economy: What Trade-Offs in an Open and Mobile Society?", Paris, 8 December 2003.

NITSCH, V. and D. SCHUMACHER (2004), "Terrorism and Trade", *European Journal of Political Economy*, forthcoming.

NORDHAUS, W.D. (2002), "The Economic Consequences of War with Iraq", *The New York Review of Books*, 49(19).

O'HANLON, M.E. et al. (2002), *Protecting the American Homeland: A Preliminary Analysis*, Brookings Institution Press, Washington DC.

PALDAM, M. and A. WÜRTZ (2003), "The Big Bend – Economic Freedom and Growth", Paper presented at the European Public Choice Society annual meeting in Aarhus.

PHILLIPS, L.T. (2001), "A Crisis of Security and Economics", *Regulation*, 24(4), pp. 53-56.

POIRSON, H. (1998), "Economic Security, Private Investment and Growth in Developing Countries", IMF Working Paper WP/98/4.

RABY, G. (2003), "The Cost of Terrorism and the Benefits of Cooperating to Combat Terrorism", Paper submitted to the Secure Trade in the APEC Region (STAR) Conference, 24 February.

SANDLER, T. (2003), "Collective Action and Transnational Terrorism", *The World Economy*, 26(6), pp. 779-802.

SANDLER, T. and W. ENDERS (2004), "An Economic Perspective on Transnational Terrorism", *European Journal of Political Economy*, forthcoming.

SHEFFI, Y. (2001), "Supply Chain Management Under the Threat of International Terrorism", *The International Journal of Logistics Management*, 12(2), pp. 1-11.

STEVENS, B. (2004), "Factors Shaping Future Demand for Security Goods and Services", in this volume and presented at the OECD Forum for the Future on "The Security Economy: What Trade-Offs in an Open and Mobile Society?", Paris, 8 December 2003.

SUNSTEIN, C.R. (2003), "Terrorism and Probability Neglect", *The Journal of Risk and Uncertainty*, 26(2/3), pp. 121-136.

TRAJTENBERG, M. (2003), "Defense R&D Policy in the Anti-Terrorist Era", NBER Working Paper Series 9725.

WALKENHORST, P. and N. DIHEL (2004), "Trade Impacts of Increased Border Security Concerns", *International Trade Journal*, forthcoming.

WOLGAST, M. and W. RUPRECHT (2003), "Weltweiter Terror und Versicherungswirtschaft: Ökonomische und politische Herausforderungen", *Ifo Schnelldienst*, 56(1), pp. 11-14.

WORLD BANK (2003), "Reducing Trading Costs in a New Era of Security", *Global Economic Prospects 2004: Realizing the Development Promise of the Doha Agenda*, pp. 179-203.

ISBN 92-64-10772-X
The Security Economy
OECD 2004

Chapter 8

Surveillance Technologies: Trends and Social Implications

by

David Lyon

Department of Sociology, Queen's University

Canada

Introduction

In the 21st century, the populations of the affluent, technologically advanced societies are not the anonymous, independent, self-directing and freely choosing persons that the dominant consumer-oriented world views and ideologies suggest. It does not take a sociologist to point out that our lives are structurally constrained by numerous circumstances, processes and practices, many of which relate to surveillance (using the broader sense of that word). We cannot enter any PIN and expect the bank machine to produce cash, board an airplane without extensive checks on our identity and our baggage, make a call from a mobile/cell phone and assume that no one will know our whereabouts, or walk out of the factory early without alerting our employers. These are, in a sense, surveillance experiences.

The aftermath of the September 11, 2001 attacks (hereafter 9/11) has had widespread ramifications for military activity and international security arrangements, but it has also raised awareness of the extensive and pervasive practices of everyday surveillance. Who gathers personal data – as well as what happens to that data – clearly has effects on our lives, both trivial and traumatic. It may be highly annoying to be spammed by marketers, but it is a major miscarriage of justice when what amounts to automated racial profiling places innocent persons under detention – or worse, torture.[1] Ordinary people may in everyday life experience either kind of unwanted attention because they live in surveillance societies.

It is important to consider the future of surveillance society but that phrase itself raises a number of questions. It assumes that "surveillance societies" exist and that something can be said about their future. According to a number of important historical and sociological research writings in the field (Rose, 1999), it is arguable that surveillance societies do indeed exist, in the sense that advanced bureaucratic and technological societies foster the detailed processing of personal data for particular purposes. And addressing their future is indeed worthwhile, as this is a rapidly expanding phenomenon. The political economy of personal information is a crucially significant area for analysis and policy, a key area of social change that has risen to prominence only in the past generation.

There are identifiable trends of which it is worth taking note, whether as ordinary citizens, workers, consumers or travellers – or, as policy makers, managers of personal data, or social and political activists. Sheer expansion of personal data processing is one trend, but it is also interesting to note some other features of surveillance. It tends to be increasingly organised using searchable databases, and is thus algorithmic and actuarial. But it also contributes increasingly to governance at a micro-social as well as macro-social level; the two are connected (Rose, 1999). A further trend is towards system integration and convergence, in which agencies processing personal information for different purposes share data according to varying protocols.

The future of surveillance societies is not a foregone conclusion.

This paper is in four main parts. The first discusses the meaning of the term surveillance society, which has gained academic and popular currency only over the past twenty years. Contemporary surveillance is here defined as the serious and systematic attention to personal details for the purposes of influence, management and control. While the new technologies are tremendously significant, it will be shown that surveillance is not merely about them; the political, economic and social-cultural context is vitally important to a proper understanding of the phenomenon. It will also be demonstrated how the aftermath of 9/11 has accelerated the growth of surveillance trends.

The second part is devoted to considering one of the most significant of these trends, what those at the Surveillance Project[2] call "social sorting" as the means to "digital discrimination". This is based on the use of searchable databases, and not only is used in an increasing number of sectors but also facilitates the use of similar methods across different, hitherto distinct sectors. The most obvious example is the use made by law enforcement of Customer Relationship Management techniques following 9/11. If surveillance involves social sorting – categorising groups for different treatment – then new forms of analysis and new responses are required.

This point is carried further in the third section, which deals with what might be thought of as the new politics of surveillance. In terms of policy and regulation, surveillance as social sorting requires either an extension of privacy concerns or a new vocabulary to mobilise appropriate responses to it. Again, however, there is a broader context to consider as well: the growth of a more general politics of information (that also touches on intellectual property rights, access, and a number of other areas) within which surveillance is located. While one important area is formal policy and regulation – in which an important emphasis is on operator accountability rather than mere user awareness – another is the emergence of new groups and social movements which have the critique of surveillance among their aims.

The fourth section turns to scenarios for the future, first suggesting a dystopian side in which present negative trends towards social sorting and a preventative approach are magnified. Human rights, data protection and privacy concerns are at a very low ebb. A more positive scenario, which some might see as utopian, follows. It does not stretch credulity to imagine a world in which matters of care regarding personal data have become much more central to organisational life. It may take some serious breach – an information Chernobyl – to bring the point home, but equally it may just be the cumulative effects of legislation and political pressure that eventually mitigate the negative aspects of today's surveillance regimes. Whatever happens, serious ethical assessment, social analysis and determined policy making will be required to minimise the chances of dystopian futures opening before us.

1. Surveillance society

Surveillance society is a real, daily phenomenon in the societies of the global north, and increasingly in the global south as well. Yet totalitarianism has not taken over, nor even authoritarianism – two systems of government usually associated with the notion of surveillance society. What, then, is meant by the term? Here it simply refers to societies in which routine, systematic and ubiquitous identifying, checking, monitoring, tracking and recording of everyday activities, communication, and exchanges have become a commonplace, unremarkable experience. Surveillance is triggered by events and behaviours in the minutiae of daily life – phone calls and cash transfers, supermarket shopping and even downtown window-shopping (under watchful cameras) – and supported by a growing infrastructure of computer systems and electronic communications, both wired and wireless.

Thus this discussion does not equate surveillance society with totalitarianism, nor even argue that it is necessarily sinister or malign. It is an aspect of the early 21st century world that has, in its present forms, been under construction for less than 20 years. Surveillance devices are installed to ensure convenience, comfort, efficiency, productivity, speed and security – none of which are normally viewed with disdain or distaste. It is not clear, of course, that any of these are basic values or primary goals, but at least they are not intrinsically undesirable, let alone evil. Surveillance practices exist along a spectrum between highly caring and highly controlling (although sometimes care will involve control, even coercion). However innocent such practices may appear, all are susceptible to ethical, social and political analysis and critique.

Examples of contemporary surveillance include the following:

- Video images of people in retail stores, transport stations, or on public streets.

- Text records in government departments, such as taxation or health.

- Personal identification numbers (PINs) that are used for a variety of purposes but particularly in financial transactions.

- Radio frequency identification (RFID) tags that may be attached to clothing by manufacturers to trace garments, but which by definition will also be associated with people wearing such garments.

- Biometric items such as face recognition, iris-scanning or fingerprint devices used in conjunction with identification (ID) cards, especially in airports or at borders.

- Navigational systems that enable vehicles to be traced or cell phones equipped for emergency location using global positioning satellite (GPS) technology; communications interception from wiretaps to Internet and email logs.

The list could go on. Of course, these items do not exist on their own. PINs and biometrics are used for identification and verification, for example, as part of larger schemes to record, track, or monitor behaviours. Surveillance as defined here covers all forms of "watching" and supervision mentioned above, as well as surveillance that involves no technological mediation. (Surveillance did not start with new technologies.) However, in modern times it has become increasingly technologically mediated, from the use of the filing cabinets of official bureaucracies to that of computerised information technologies that were developed in the later 20th century. It is within *systems* of surveillance that the individual items discussed here become significant.

Just as such systems include specific devices for identification, so surveillance systems themselves are part of larger entities. More specifically, they are an important aspect of what we today call "governance". This is very important, because associating surveillance society and technologies can be misleading in the extreme. On the one hand, any designation of a society can suggest that its *overriding* feature is in the modifier – in this case, *surveillance* society. Worse, it can hint that an entirely new social formation, a radically novel epoch, has dawned. In actual fact, the situation is much murkier and more muddled than a neat phrase like "surveillance society" suggests. On the other hand, the emphasis on new technologies can also give many misleading impressions. Two major examples of such mistakes are that social changes are caused by technological development, and that the technologies can be discussed unambiguously either as a class – say, information technology or biotechnology – or in terms of their efficacy.

To speak of surveillance society is merely a rhetorical device to draw attention to a particular aspect of the contemporary world, albeit one that has become more socially significant in recent decades. The concept of surveillance becomes a lens with which to view social relationships (just as "street corner society", "risk society" and "network society" are lenses). But the concept is neither self-contained nor self-defining. Surveillance societies can only be understood in terms of much broader political-economic and cultural changes that occurred during the 20th century. Indeed it is no accident that the term only appeared the 1980s, from the pens (or possibly typewriters) of historians (Flaherty, 1989) and sociologists[3] who felt that they could discern unprecedented alterations in the social and political landscape that boded ill for conventional understandings of the role of the state, and of law enforcement in particular. The use of the concept of surveillance is even more justified today; not only the state and agencies of law enforcement but also commercial enterprises and indeed ordinary people in everyday life are also involved in surveillance practices.

To speak of technologies, on the other hand, is to indicate how surveillance practices are mediated. Surveillance may include all kinds of non-technological mediations, but the kinds of surveillance that are especially prominent today are technically-based. While mutual watching of villagers or townsfolk was the rule in traditional societies, supplemented periodically by specific state or religious oversight, surveillance became much more centralised with modernity. This occurred in bureaucratic organisations of the nation-state, the military, and the capitalist corporation (Dandeker, 1990; Higgs, 2001). The information technologies of bureaucracy were the main mechanisms of surveillance until the later 1960s. At that point computerisation helped broaden surveillance to other areas and new telecommunications provided the means behind what we know today – automated and networked surveillance systems.

The question of technology is critically important. While it is a big mistake to imagine that technology could ever be a driver of social change, technologies nonetheless do make a big difference, for several reasons. The political economy of surveillance technologies is one in which major companies are competing fiercely for contracts within the context of new post-9/11 security industries. Globalisation means that similar processes are in train in many countries at once, and there is also pressure to harmonise systems in the hope of achieving maximum security. Socially, there is a widespread acceptance of many new surveillance technologies, close cousins of which are often first introduced in consumer or workplace contexts. And culturally, there is an increasing willingness to permit automation in areas once exclusively the province of face-to-face activity, such as screening at national border control points. When, for all these reasons and more, new technologies become the means of mediating surveillance, they do have substantial effects. For instance, computer records are treated with more respect than personal accounts. Old thresholds of acceptable profiling are transcended. And management starts to substitute for morality.

Now let us put these two together: the surveillance society today depends upon new technologies. That is an innocent-sounding assertion (first intimated in Marx, 1988), even though its ramifications may give pause to readers of Franz Kafka, George Orwell and Margaret Atwood.[4] The mistake is to imagine that surveillance society is somehow constituted by those technologies. The surveillance society is one in which certain kinds of watching, both literal and (more often) figurative, have become the preferred means of maintaining – indeed creating – social order. These scopic and informational regimes are enabled by electronic technologies, but it is their social and cultural implications that are really significant. To automate control, as Michalis Lianos and Mary Douglas point out (2000), is to create non-negotiable contexts of interaction (you cannot do anything about a PIN that will not work), turn "law-abiding citizens" into "efficient users", and displace class distinctions while nonetheless favouring specific power relationships (those of the institutions using them).

When we analyse the power relationships relating to the multitude of institutions now using forms of automated control, we perceive the importance of *governance*. The idea of governance really takes off from Michel Foucault's work on "governmentality" and is used to examine a plethora of technologies of power and strategies of control that now govern our conduct from day to day. It also relates to actual changes taking place since the 1970s, in which the state's role has been downplayed in favour of both market mechanisms and other agencies, from the level of local civil society through to transnational organisations operating at a global level.

This takes the focus off any one institution as such (*e.g.* the nation-state), and instead uses a wide-angle lens to take in the range and complexity of control mechanisms and their appearance in hitherto unfamiliar locations. So, far from resembling the old top-down pyramidal structure of totalitarian states – or some neat new technological mega-machine – this is a loose-knit, fluctuating, fragmentary and contested arena of control. Richard Ericson and Kevin Haggerty (2000) call it the "surveillant assemblage" (after Gilles Deleuze). For them, the key is to see how the individual body is broken down into bits of data for collection, storage and retrieval. These may be through commercial transactions such as credit card swipes, or digitised images such as those on new passports. They are raw materials for the production of identities that proxy for persons within current circuits of control.

Of course, the idea that governance or the assemblage involves no one centre, or that it is contradictory and flexible, does not mean that no patterns can be discerned within it. Nikolas Rose (2000), for example, argues that contemporary control strategies can be divided into two main "families": those that regulate individuals by "enmeshing" them in circuits of inclusion, and those that act on pathologies through managing circuits of exclusion. Of the former, Rose suggests that the best examples are identification documents such as driver's licences and passports. These yield a virtual identity and link the bearer to a database, while at the same time offering access to privileges and entitlements. After 9/11, they have become even more significant (and controversial) as numerous new cards are proposed and implemented to fast-track passengers through airports or to provide tamper-proof evidence that the bearer is not a security risk. This is linked with a widening sense of personal responsibility for safety and with an expanding divide between "safe" and "unsafe" spaces.

Circuits of exclusion, meanwhile, are reserved for those who, for whatever reason, fail to manage their own well-being and security, or who are thought of as risky individuals. Rather than considering their discipline or reform, this approach merely regulates levels of deviance. It is managerial and to some extent actuarial in style. While the poor, homeless, and unemployed may be its usual targets, dramatic upsurges may occur at particular times – the aftermath of 9/11 being a key example. It is consistent with the exclusionary strategy to regard some as particularly dangerous; the high profile of post-9/11 suspects can eclipse the ongoing processes of exclusion especially evident in the United Kingdom and the United States. As in the case of inclusionary strategies, new technologies of surveillance are the means of gathering information on which classifications and judgements may be made on a case-by-case basis.

Before turning to some of the characteristics of today's surveillance, it is worth commenting on some of the cultural consequences of the governance modes that depend on that surveillance, especially since 9/11. Three in particular come to mind: the development of cultures of fear, suspicion, and secrecy.

Fear is a significant feature, if not general condition, of today's cultural terrain (Glassner, 1999). In the consumer context, retailers fear the supposed loss of trade that occurs when homeless people or teenagers hang around their stores, and support street video surveillance as a means of discouraging them. Some ordinary pedestrians in downtown cores have imbibed the lurid lore of local newspapers and television such that they too fear to walk those streets designated as dangerous.

Underlying the quest for consumer surveillance equipment, now readily available in stores and on the Internet, is the desire to be free from fear. Fear is a dominant factor in many domestic and neighbourhood concerns in the 21st century. One can buy peace of mind, apparently, by purchasing items such as "nanny-cams" with which children in daycare may be watched from a "window" in the corner of the parental workplace computer screen. (This also functions as a form of surveillance over daycare workers, of course.) One may even pick up a handy device sold as a "techno-bra" to instantly detect sexual assault and raise an alarm. Much surveillance equipment is sold as a means of allaying fears and quieting the anxieties of those who ignore statistical realities about assault and abuse and read only the headlines of peril and hazard.

On a societal level, fear has become a dominant motif since 9/11. Here is fear of an elusive "enemy within" whose racialised characteristics have produced an unprecedented suspension of civil liberties that includes the widespread use of new surveillance technologies to create categories of suspicion (Parenti, 2003; Lyon, 2003a). Fears have been fanned, no doubt unintentionally, by the establishment of upgraded security arrangements, the relentless references to orange and red alerts, and by the constant admonitions to ordinary citizens to become the eyes and ears of the agencies of policing and law enforcement. Such "eyes and ears" are intended to work in conjunction with the fully fledged systems of intelligence and surveillance whose budgets have burgeoned since the fateful events of 9/11.

All this takes place, as argued earlier, within cultural contexts where fear is a significant factor. Fear is many-faceted, and also ebbs and flows as histories and biographies intersect, here fomented by media amplification, there mitigated by communal involvement, commitments, and clear-sightedness. Our societies are, as Frank Furedi (1997) says, fearful because "[...] the evaluation of everything from the perspective of safety is a defining characteristic". We perceive the world as dangerous, do not trust others, and are sceptical about whether any intervention might work. Yet the kinds of fear discussed here are specific, to environments (such as airports, streets) and particular classes of persons (prostitutes, drug addicts, homeless people, "terrorists" and so on). While there may be a general "culture of fear", it is important to specify what sorts of fear are significant, in what places, for which persons, and at what times (Tudor, 2002).

If cultures of fear are a significant cause and effect of growing surveillance regimes, then these are closely related to cultures of suspicion. The term is used by Onora O'Neill in her 2002 book A Question of Trust and is used by the author to describe one of the chief results of the aftermath of 9/11. It ties in closely with the governance theme, in which all kinds of agencies, some far removed from law enforcement, engage in surveillance practices. In the post-9/11 case, however, there are many governmental encouragements to keep close watch, and also an expectation that personal information will be passed to agencies of law enforcement and security. Fear fosters suspicion of strangers in general [from potential paedophiles to anyone who appears to be "out of place"[5] (Norris and Armstrong, 1999)] but after 9/11 suspicion was particularised to persons of "Middle-Eastern" or "Arab" appearance. Many calls have been made to hotlines set up after 9/11, and much information has been voluntarily handed over to law enforcement agencies by private citizens and by corporations.

In addition to the materials passed to law enforcement agencies, however, personal data have also been used for forms of security check internal to organisations. Thus for example, corporations hire consultants and private detectives to run risk-threat checks on applicants for positions, and credit card companies have refused to re-activate accounts of persons with suspicious names. In these cases, no data are passed to authorities; the processes of inclusion and exclusion are carried out within the nongovernmental and non-police organisations concerned. Already existing cultures of suspicion have rippled out further in ways that both directly bolster the activities of law enforcement and create colonies of control in areas hitherto unassociated with the formal mechanisms of maintaining social order.

The cultures of fear connected with the drive for tightened security and their stimulus to suspicion, expressed in widening waves of personal data gathering, exist in a climate of growing secrecy. Information sources have been shut down in the name of security, and it has become increasingly difficult to learn exactly what happens to personal information on suspect lists, or indeed to the persons to whom the information refers. Thus a third culture, that of secrecy, is currently evident in any country attempting to deal with the aftermath of 9/11.

This culture is of course deepened by the events of 9/11, whereas fear and suspicion tend to accompany much contemporary surveillance, before as well as after 9/11. Similar to the McCarthy era in the United States, all sorts of persons have become suspect. Any form of "anti-American" or "anti-corporate" sentiment, including anti-globalisation protest and trade unionism, may be viewed by some on a continuum with violence and sedition. Knowledge of which groups are targeted is frequently withheld; those whose personal data are collected are not informed that they are under suspicion. Indeed, the data are often gathered in ways that are far from transparent, and passed from one police agency to another across national borders. Thus the web-surfing activities of World Trade Organization protesters who had used the Internet to prepare for the demonstration in Seattle were passed to the Royal Canadian Mounted Police, so that they would be checked carefully before crossing the border for the Quebec City protests of 2002.

As suggested above, all three cultures were already present long before 9/11. Fear and suspicion in particular have a symbiotic relationship with new technologies of surveillance. These not only expose details of personal life to a range of agencies to which they are valuable, but also automate the process of classification and categorisation. Discriminating between one person and another on the basis of a computer profile or data image is achieved through a process that can usefully be thought of as "social sorting".

2. Surveillance as social sorting

Human beings have always discriminated and been the objects of discrimination. This is an unremarkable feature of daily life. We are sorted into age groups at high school and later classified according to competences, nationality, credentials and so on. There is an element of randomness to every such sorting, but we are usually aware of the criteria on which decisions are made. So if one is in dispute – a diploma, a city of birth, a question of age – it can be resolved with our informed intervention. The means to make the assessment are publicly accessible and we are aware of the difference it makes to be classified, one way or another.

In the 21st century, however, discrimination has become automated. The upshot is that the processes of categorisation have become relatively opaque as they are computerised. Where advanced information infrastructures exist, they are used to do the task of classification. The key to this, as Lawrence Lessig pointed out very clearly in his *Code and Other Laws of Cyberspace* (1999), is searchable databases. Personal data can be stored in a form amenable to automatic sorting on the basis of any given criterion, or several criteria, so that one class of persons may easily be distinguished from another. The more personal details are collected, and the more different databases can be linked together, the more fine-grained – at least in principle – the resulting profile will be. This is the "Google" model of surveillance, where apparently limitless permutations are possible, as the name "googol" suggests.[6]

Access to improved speed of handling and to richer resources of information about individuals and populations is thought to be the best way to check and monitor behaviour, to influence persons and groups, and to anticipate and pre-empt risks. The classic sector in which such social sorting has developed is not law enforcement or government administration (though data from these are used), but marketing. A huge industry has mushroomed over the past two or three decades, devoted to clustering populations according to geodemographic type. In Canada, a company called Compusearch organises the population data into groups, from U1 for Urban Elite to R2 for Rural Downscale, and subdivides them into smaller clusters. U1 includes the "affluentials" cluster: "Very affluent and middle-aged executive and professional families. Expensive, large, lightly mortgaged houses in older, exclusive sections of larger cities. Older children and teenagers."[7] U6, "Big City Stress" is rather different: "Inner city urban neighbourhoods with second lowest average household income. Probably the most disadvantaged areas of the country... Household types include singles, couples, and lone-parent families. A significant but mixed 'ethnic' presence. Unemployment levels are very high."

These clusters are used in conjunction with postal codes (or zip codes in the United States) to sift and sort populations according to their spending patterns, and then treat different clusters accordingly. Groups valuable to marketers are offered higher quality service, better deals and special attention, while those whose data profile suggests that they will not spend so much make do with less information, inferior service and less attractive offers. Thus customers are classified according to their relative worth to the company, using whatever indicators are available or can be found. The sales clerk may well know not only where the individual lives, and what sort(s) of lifestyle he or she has, but also items such as ethnic background [in the United States Acxiom matches names with demographic data to yield B for black, J for Jewish, and N for Japanese (Stepanek, 2000)].

When the customer is asked for a phone number or postcode at the checkout desk, this is the reason why. As the customer stands there their details are recorded in order to rate their worth to the company from whom they are making purchases. In 2003 a UK newspaper reported how this process occurs in call centres. When the customer call comes through for ordering products or after-sales service, the incoming calls are automatically routed to different operators based on the postal code revealed by the caller's telephone number. Those calls originating in high-end postal code zones are sent to operators trained to offer high quality service, the best discounts, and most information. Calls from people whose postcode-generated status is low are routed to a voice that offers the "next available agent" who, if the customer waits, will attempt to clear the line as swiftly as possible (*Sunday Times*, 2003).

Other uses are made of searchable databases and their clustering potential, including policing, attempts to root out welfare and social benefits fraud and, now, anti-terrorism (Lyon, 2003b, especially Chapter 1). With regard to the latter, it is interesting to note that law enforcement agencies called first upon marketers to help them build systems to profile potential "terrorists". Customer Relationship Management, one of the chief database marketing techniques, itself found a new market niche after 9/11 (Lyon, 2003c). Within each sector, the trend is towards prediction and pre-emption of behaviours and, some even claim, towards "actuarial justice" in which communication of knowledge about probabilities plays a growing role in assessments of risk (Ericson and Haggerty, 1997). Similar methods lie behind efforts to produce reliable facial recognition and other biometrics-based systems, all of which have gained a much higher public profile since 9/11.

The simple point to be made from the exploration of social sorting is that organisational identities that have proliferated during the modern era have now become much more sophisticated, and have increasing social effects. All of us are linked through our personal data with numerous organisations and agencies (some we are conscious of, others not) in a complex and ever-changing web of relations. In the new climate, "private" data such as property ownership, Internet domains and cell phone numbers are increasingly interfaced with "public" data of law enforcement. Risk has become more individualised in the political-economic restructuring of the past three decades, and with this process, categorising and clustering of risky profiles have increased. Individual choices and life-chances are determined in relation to risk assessments and profitability analyses, with the result that social sorting is a powerful means of discrimination between different classes of persons. In a sense, it helps to create new social classes, constituted not merely by the conventional measures of occupation and income, but also by analyses of lifestyles and consumption patterns as well.

This process of increasing social sorting is not in itself malign (we readily allow ourselves to be sorted for many purposes, from bathroom use to theatre seating to airport queues), but it does contribute to potential tyranny as well as increased democratisation. As Geoff Bowker and Susan Leigh Star observe (1999), it is all too easy for infrastructure builders to build their politics into their systems, as well as allowing bureaucratic inertia (red tape) or organisational complexity to reign by default. This theme has been picked up by social analysts: *inter alia*, Oscar Gandy with regard to marketing, Clive Norris in relation to video surveillance, Steve Graham in analyses of urban infrastructure and services, and Richard Jones with particular referencing to policing and control. Similar techniques are used in quite different contexts, but this also permits increased convergence between systems – a fact that has been exploited especially within the Department of Homeland Security in the United States.

Social sorting is also facilitated by the use of universal identifiers, such as the smart national ID cards that are being tested or implemented in a number of countries in the early 21st century. Although such cards do not inevitably contribute to the risks of unfair discrimination, given the purposes for which they are rolled out – to combat illegal immigration, welfare fraud, terrorist activity, anti-globalisation protests, drug trafficking and the like – it would be surprising if some rather prejudicial profiling did not result from their use. Social sorting is made easier each time a common identifier, whether driver's licence, postcode, social insurance number or ID card, is used. It offers further opportunities for matching and linking data, which in turned may be mined and otherwise manipulated to discriminate between groups and offer differential treatment based on automated assessments.

3. Surveillance politics

Data protection and privacy dominate the discourse of "surveillance society" debates. There is only slow recognition of the social nature and consequences of categorisation, and thus the need for greater transparency and accountability. There are threats to privacy, and these are important. There is an ethics that relates to the communication of personal data – "self-disclosure", in other words – which says that people should be permitted to communicate information about themselves in ways that are voluntary, limited, and based on relations of trust (or, better, covenant). Such ideas lie behind fair information principles, which have become basic to data protection and privacy legislation and policy around the world.

Yet there is more here than can be adequately covered by the term "privacy". There are issues such as the abuse of data mining; risk profiling and social sorting; discrimination and exacerbation of inequalities. There are also cross-border flows of personal data: risks of mistakes, misuse of information in categorising, and so on. It is true that privacy and data protection law can cover these kinds of issues (see for example Bennett and Raab, 2003) but the question is whether they can do so satisfactorily. Privacy is a useful mobilising slogan in individualistic societies, where the first question is "What difference does it make to me?" But the kinds of issues discussed here are irreducibly social ones, and it is difficult to cover all the issues raised by reference to a concept whose development has been mainly individualistic.[8]

A classic error is repeated endlessly in numerous contexts, and it reveals the depth of misunderstanding that surrounds surveillance today. The claim is frequently made that if we have done nothing wrong, we have nothing to hide, and thus nothing to fear. The principle is an excellent one, of course. Western jurisprudence has encouraged us to believe in the presumption of innocence, in due process, and in the idea that only when someone has been proved guilty in court will the appropriate punishment be meted out. The problem is that this is not how things work, especially in the context of surveillance as social sorting, as an aspect of a complex assemblage of governance practices. Against the personal claims of individual innocence, surveillance practices are profoundly social, in the sense that persons are clustered into categories, whether of potential consumer groups or potential lawbreakers. It is one's often unwitting membership of or association with certain groupings that makes all the difference. And the more systems are integrated and cross-referenced, the more it becomes possible to create categories in which to capture personal information that lead to the singling out of a person as a risk threat, a suspect, or a target.

This is why the politics of surveillance are starting to change – and why, if the potentially negative aspects of surveillance are to be constrained, they must change. An increasing range of studies show that the focus on individual intrusions and on breaches of confidentiality is inadequate to the task. Privacy issues, classically construed, are important, but to focus only on these is to turn a blind eye to questions of controlling the use of personal data. The larger questions have to do with how systems are coded, who creates the categories, and what are the consequences of such social sorting for ordinary people.

The reason why this is likely to become a battleground is that the forces ranged to collect and process personal data are increasingly powerful ones. Commercial surveillance of consumers is now a billion dollar multinational business. Huge profits are made not merely in amassing and processing personal data but also in trading them. And governments, too, continue to collect data for specific departments, but also to facilitate systems – such as e-government – whose surveillance dimensions are little understood or even acknowledged. But the same system that works with a universal identifier and offers opportunities for access to government information and services also offers opportunities for unprecedented monitoring and profiling of population groups and individuals.

Since 9/11, one process in particular is being augmented: that of facilitating the cross-linking of commercial and government or law enforcement databases. This was already apparent in areas such as E911 and similar services that make cell phones with GPS capacities the means of emergency contact. In the United Kingdom, the Regulation of Investigatory Powers Act (2000, thus antedating 9/11) also has such cross-linking capacities. But the Computer-Assisted Passenger Pre-Screening program (CAPPS II) and other similar initiatives simply take further such cross-sector interactions. This is why the aftermath of 9/11 is such a critical moment for the development of a new politics of information, appropriate to the emergent dimensions of the issue.

However that issue is resolved in the long term, the question remains: What is the best approach to curb the spread of unwarranted and negative aspects of contemporary surveillance? Regulation is one approach among others, and this is moving in the healthy direction of seeking greater accountability among those who process personal data. Such an approach has always been more characteristic of European than North American regulatory regimes, although one could argue that with the PIPEDA (Personal Information Protection and Electronic Documents Act), which came fully into force on 1 January 2004, a shift in this direction is also discernible in Canada.[9] Improved legislation is vital for creating a culture of care about personal data, and for resisting the voracious and insatiable appetite for them which is encouraged by cultures of fear and suspicion as well as by corporate cultures addicted to targeted marketing.

In the 21st century, however, as the politics of information is moving to a more central position, other players such as new social movements, NGOs and consumer and Internet groups are becoming aware of its significance. Signs are that the post-9/11 climate is serving to alert broader groups to the questions raised by surveillance, and these are also tied in with other kinds of initiative. Anti-globalisation movements are starting to see surveillance as an important dimension of public policy, and these frequently operate across national boundaries. Such transnational developments are to be welcomed, but they do raise several more questions about how far the cultures of surveillance and privacy are the same across different nations, cultures and ethnic groups. The globalisation of personal data is a process that can only be understood and confronted on fronts that are at once local and global.[10]

Key questions are raised of security versus democratic liberties; of efficiency versus less control over personal information; of where governments should regulate and the consequences of doing so. In the first issue, the media rhetoric has constantly offered security and democratic liberties as alternatives rather than things that can be pursued in a complementary fashion. In the second, the notion of efficiency has usurped proper social goals, to suggest that control over personal information is somehow an equivalent value. And in the third, government regulation is often thought of as the key institution for regulation, whereas many opportunities also exist for local organisations and agencies to regulate themselves *within a framework* enshrined in law. Given the discussion so far, that shows both the pervasiveness of new social sorting techniques and their relative opaqueness to so-called data subjects, it is vital that the politics of information be joined as a public debate over matters of life-chances and of choices.

4. Surveillance scenarios

Having stated his scepticism about scenarios that attempt somehow to foretell the future, it is nonetheless incumbent on the author to suggest possible directions in which current trends are taking us. The foolish dream that sociology might be able to predict the future has, it appears, been put to rest. Certainly no sociologist forecast that 1989 would be the decisive year for dismantling Communism, or that 2001 would be remembered for an attack on New York and Washington. However, simply by describing current events, and placing them within a meaningful sequence which suggests a trend, some sense may be made of the claim that sociology can suggest alternatives. Two will be presented here: one dystopian, the other more hopeful.

Let us begin with the dystopian. Today's world is not, in most cases, *Nineteen Eighty-Four*, although it must be said that no responsible surveillance scenario ought to ignore that classic case. George Orwell noted many crucially important features of surveillance societies, and placed them in the context of human beings' common decency to one another, and the basic insight that truth-telling is vital to a healthy society (Slater, 2003). But he could not have foreseen the extent to which non-state organisations would become involved in the practices of everyday governance, or the developments in technology that would, for example, permit authorities to use searchable databases to create categories of suspicion. His social ethical instincts were good ones, and he cannot be faulted for not second-guessing political and technological developments. But we must go beyond Orwell – and some Orwellian clichés such as Big Brother – if we are to grasp the elements of a 21st century surveillance dystopia.

If situational crime control and database marketing have become as significant as suggested earlier, then these would have to be the key features of the dystopian future. They are not dystopian merely because the new technologies have apparently "taken over" and perhaps threaten to bump humans from some key decision-making roles, but because of the deeper trends that are made visible here. The mere fact of using new technologies is not itself the cause of threat. Rather, the role that they are permitted to play raises questions about the viability of a human future. As we have seen, fragments of personal data are now concatenated to create proxies for the human subjects to whom their identifiers refer. For many practical purposes those images and profiles that proxy for persons are taken to be sufficient for determining treatments. This bypasses more conventional notions of accountability and responsibility; morality is superseded by management.

One could well ask if, in the early 21st century, a threshold is being crossed from which it may become very difficult to return. Of course, the relationship of citizens and states constantly undergoes minor modification, and already in the later 20th century the relation altered somewhat as citizens started to relate to an amorphous "global" as well as a state reality. It does seem, for example with the introduction of fingerprinting for many non-Americans at US border points, that this threshold is being reached, as body-data count for more than conventional personal narratives and portable documents. The US case is simply a well-publicised one; the process may be seen in many other national contexts. The human body, which for a very long time was assumed to be intimately associated and inextricably bound up with the person, is now seen as a reliable source of data in its own right, such that entry may be permitted or denied on its basis. Such bodies-without-voices are dubiously and disturbingly placed in terms of conventional politics.

At the same time, technological fixes rule supreme. This is the key means of preventing the ineligible or the risky from gaining access to sites or experiences. In each case the complexity of persons is reduced to data-images, justice to the actuarial, morality to management. The culture of control, with its tendencies either to manage or to demonise the alleged offender, is writ large in the post-9/11 security environment. As David Garland (2001) argues, these are key tendencies in the contemporary United Kingdom and United States, where situational crime control using surveillance (among other things) is probably more advanced than anywhere else in the world. These are not dystopian trends for the naïve reasons that technologies are "in control" or that attempts to reduce crime levels are fundamentally flawed. Rather, they are dystopian because technological and managerial approaches are preferred over ones that acknowledge the person or the claims of justice.

If these kinds of trends do indeed continue unchecked, we shall find ourselves increasingly in a world that we do not recognise – or relish. Fear, secrecy, and suspicion are burgeoning, as new technologies are seen as saviours. (Witness the number of high-tech companies that call themselves "***** Solutions".) Again, the quest for technological assistance is not itself mistaken. Rather, the problem is the apparent unwillingness of many governments and companies to submit to scrutiny new practices and processes that may well lubricate a slide into very undesirable social and political situations. Indeed, they reduce opportunities for the development of the social, and shrivel the realm of the political.

An alternative scenario could be described as "utopian". That term is used here to signify a preferred and not impossible future that arises from present conditions. Many utopias posit some cataclysm or revolution that divides the old world from the new, and perhaps our alternative scenario should do something similar. One fears for what this might be, but it is unfortunately the case that regulation and legislation do not occur until people die, however cogent and compelling the prior warnings.

There is no reason why popular outcry and serious political momentum against the negative aspects of surveillance should not rise to huge proportions without the intervention of a personal data Chernobyl, but if such a cataclysm does occur one can hope that its damage will be very limited. The new surveillance containment mood would fit with the unease that led to the curtailing of TIA and CAPPS II in the United States in 2003. Organisations committed to containing the spread of unnecessary surveillance and opposed to its abuses are already working together much more significantly, particularly following a number of global gatherings in which the interests of both responsible corporations and popular groups represented by NGOs have been discussed in the first few years of the 21st century. There are already signs that some organisations are taking far more care with personal information, especially of more sensitive kinds; as alertness to the vulnerability of personal data grows, this could be a feature of large organisations and government departments as well. Personal data audits are already carried out routinely within organisations, and cross-border agreements on the migration of personal data are leading to much tighter limitations on which data may be passed from one jurisdiction to another.

A further feature of the hopeful, utopian scenario would be that ethical scrutiny and democratic participation occur in the process of devising new surveillance systems. Information and computer scientists already sometimes work together with social analysts and policy makers to ensure that coding is done in ethically appropriate ways and that categories are transparent not only to data-users but to data-subjects. This is an area for tremendous growth in the so-called information societies of the 21st century. Educational initiatives, too, could ensure that a computer literacy programme include as crucial component skills development, not only in handling and accessing data but also in the sensitive handling of all forms of personal information. Because so many people at both ends of the social scale have started to see how their lives are affected by surveillance, chances are good that legislation will be heeded and compliance high. Some may even start to contemplate a time when low-tech is considered as desirable as high-tech and social goals are promoted above economic ones.

Each of the above will differ, of course, depending on national contexts and cultural conditions. Needs and expectations vary, but it is possible to find common ground, as experience with the European Data Protection Directive has shown.

5. Conclusions

Surveillance is a key issue for social and political analysis in the early 21st century. It is also a crucial arena for ethical scrutiny and for policy debate. It takes its place within a larger politics of information that promises to expand as organisations come increasingly to depend on informational infrastructures. But the political economy of information that frames this also has to be understood. Information, and above all personal information, has become immensely valuable both to corporations seeking to construct customers for their products and for governments concerned about the adequacy of their security arrangements, especially since 9/11. Because these two very powerful entities are pushing hard for access to ever-increasing sources of digital data – and because where their interests coincide they collude to promote them – it is clear that the struggle to ensure that sufficient safeguards are in place to protect persons will be severe.

As stated in the Introduction, the future of surveillance societies is by no means a foregone conclusion. What actually happens from day to day is not the result of some technological fate or some relentless social process. Though this is not the place to discuss the matter, the technologies are often compromised or limited in their capacity to fulfil the promises made on their behalf. Organisations are governed by many other factors in addition to bureaucratic rationality. Human beings – those abstracted by the term "data-subjects" – are knowledgeable and reflexive, fully capable of intelligent response to the growth of surveillance systems, particularly when the latter appear to operate in unfair or inappropriate ways. So much, in other words, is contingent, that no definitive forecasts about surveillance societies are either possible or desirable. At the same time, standing back to take a long-term view of where discernible trends seem to be leading is worthwhile.

Positively, this means that every effort should be made both to understand and to intervene in surveillance societies, on multiple levels. More research is required to follow through the implications of surveillance expansion, especially in areas involving biometrics, genetics, universal identifiers, video (CCTV) and locational devices (GPS, RFID), along with the growing cross-border traffic in personal data for both law-enforcement and commercial purposes. Ethical and policy research is also vital as a background to how governments and other authorities should debate attempts to regulate personal data flows – again, especially after 9/11. Educational initiatives are also required, both at a general level within high schools and universities and (especially) within university departments of computer and information science, to encourage contextual understanding of everyday processes involving personal information. Action will also be taken by groups and organisations, at very local as well as far-flung global scales, to work towards environments for handling personal data that are marked by technological prudence and a keen sense of fairness and openness.

While the future of the surveillance society may not be a foregone conclusion, present directions suggest that urgent, concerted and informed action will have to be taken on a number of fronts to harness surveillance power for humane and just purposes, and thus to preclude the possibility that it creates as many risks as it sets out to limit. While there are palpable risks to be faced – yes, with the aid of technology – in the unstable globalised world of the 21st century, it must be seen that these risks include ones that are technologically mediated and augmented. Companies and governments must come to realise that nothing important is lost, and much that is vital could be gained, by attending carefully to the social and political consequences of automating personal data processing. The future of liveable democratic societies will depend in part on seeing questions of data protection and civil liberties as more than mere noise in the process of selling technologies and promoting security.

Notes

1. Canadian Maher Arar, detained in jail for 374 days after being deported to Syria after mistakenly being identified as an al-Qaeda activist, is a case in point. He was allegedly tortured. His case is one of many such, around the world.

2. The Surveillance Project is a social science-based research initiative at Queen's University in Kingston, Ontario, Canada (currently funded 2000-2007).

3. It seems the term was first used by Gary T. Marx, in 1985.

4. The author has in mind such salutary novels as *The Trial*, *Nineteen Eighty-Four* and *The Handmaid's Tale*.

5. Being "out of place" is a common justification used, for example, in public video surveillance schemes.

6. Googol is a number equal to 1 followed by a hundred zeros.

7. "Psyte Market Segments" by TETRAD : *www.tetrad.com/pcensus/com/py951st.html*.

8. But on this point see the work of Priscilla Regan (1995), who argues that privacy itself can only be understood properly in terms of its social dimensions.

9. But see *e.g.* Chris Conrath, "Privacy Clock Strikes Midnight" ITWorld Canada.com, *www.itworld.ca/Pages/Docbase/ViewArticle/aspx?id=idgml-5f6a819b-3e80-4bd2-bc04-9be18fc69103*.

10. The current major programme of the Surveillance Project at Queen's is an international collaborative study, from social science and policy perspectives, of the Globalisation of Personal Data.

Bibliography

BENNETT, Colin and Charles RAAB (2003), *The Governance of Privacy*, Ashgate, London.

BOWKER, Geoffrey C. and Susan Leigh STAR (1999), *Sorting Things Out: Classification and Its Consequences*, MIT Press, Cambridge, Massachusetts.

DANDEKER, Christopher (1990), *Surveillance Power and Modernity*, Polity Press, Cambridge.

ERICSON, Richard and Kevin HAGGERTY (1997), *Policing the Risk Society*, University of Toronto Press, Toronto.

ERICSON, Richard and Kevin HAGGERTY (2000), "The Surveillant Assemblage", *British Journal of Sociology*, 51 (3).

FLAHERTY, David (1989), *Protecting Privacy in Surveillance Societies*, University of North Carolina Press, Chapel Hill.

FUREDI, Frank (1997), *Culture of Fear: Risk-Taking and the Morality of Low Expectation*, Cassel, London and Washington, p. 4.

GARLAND, David (2001), *The Culture of Control*, University of Chicago Press, Chicago.

GLASSNER, Barry (1999), *The Culture of Fear: Why Americans are Afraid of the Wrong Things*, Basic Books, New York.

HIGGS, Eric (2001), "The Rise of State Surveillance in England", *Journal of Historical Sociology*.

LESSIG, Lawrence (1999), *Code and Other Laws of Cyberspace*, Basic Books, New York.

LIANOS, Michalis and Mary DOUGLAS (2000), "Dangerization and the End of Deviance: The Institutional Environment" in David Garland and Richard Sparks (eds.), *Criminology and Social Theory*, Oxford University Press, Oxford.

LYON, David (2003a), *Surveillance After September 11*, Blackwell, Malden; Polity Press, Cambridge.

LYON, David, ed. (2003b), *Surveillance as Social Sorting: Privacy, Risk, and Digital Discrimination*, Routledge, London and New York.

LYON, David (2003c), "Technology *vs*. Terrorism", *International Journal of Urban and Regional Research*, 27 (3), pp. 666-678.

MARX, Gary T. (1988), *Undercover: Police Surveillance in America*, University of California Press, Berkeley.

NORRIS, Clive and Gary ARMSTRONG (1999), *Towards the Maximum Security Society*, Berg, London.

O'NEILL, Onora (2002), *A Question of Trust*, Cambridge University Press, Cambridge.

PARENTI, Christian (2003), The Soft Cage: Surveillance in America from Slavery to the War on Terror, Basic Books, New York.

REGAN, Priscilla (1995), *Legislating Privacy*, University of North Carolina Press, Chapel Hill.

ROSE, Nikolas (1999), *Powers of Freedom*, Cambridge University Press, Cambridge.

ROSE, Nikolas (2000), "Government and Control" in D. Garland and R. Sparks (eds.), *Criminology and Social Theory*, Oxford University Press, Oxford, pp. 183-208.

SLATER, Ian (2003), *Orwell: The Road to Airstrip One*, McGill-Queens University Press.

STEPANEK, M. (2000), "Weblining", Business Week, 3 April, *www.businessweek.com:/2000/00_14/b3675027.htm/*.

SUNDAY TIMES (2003), "Are You a Second Class Consumer?", 9 October.

TUDOR, Andrew (2002), "A (Macro) Sociology of Fear?", *The Sociological Review*, 51(2).

ISBN 92-64-10772-X
The Security Economy
OECD 2004

ANNEX

List of Participants

Chairman: **Michael OBORNE**
Director, Advisory Unit to the Secretary-General, OECD

Francis ALDHOUSE
Deputy Information Commissioner
United Kingdom

David BAXTER
Director, Strategic Relations, Group Technology & Engineering
BT Group
United Kingdom

Andrew BRIDGES
Attorney at Law
Wilson Sonsini Goodrich & Rosati
United States

Tilman BRÜCK
Head, Department of International Economics
German Institute for Economic Research (DIW Berlin)
Germany

Dagfinn BUSET
Adviser, Emergency Planning Unit
Rescue and Emergency Planning Department
Norwegian Ministry of Justice and the Police
Norway

Anne CARBLANC
Information, Security & Privacy
Directorate for Science, Technology & Industry
OECD

Lutz CLEEMANN
Managing Director
Allianz Zentrum für Technik GmbH
Germany

Shana DALE
Chief of Staff and General Counsel
Office of Science and Technology Policy
Executive Office of the President
Unites States

Bernard DIDIER
Director, Technical and Business Development
SAGEM Security Division
SAGEM SA
France

Manuel HEITOR
Professor, Department of Mechanical Engineering
Centre for Innovation, Technology and Policy Research
Portugal

Steve HODGES
Technical Director Europe
Auto-ID Lab
Institute for Manufacturing
Cambridge University Engineering Dept.
United Kingdom

Kevin HURST
Policy Analyst, Office of Science and Technology Policy
Executive Office of the President
United States

Urho ILMONEN
Director, Corporate Relations and Chief Security Officer
NOKIA Corporation
Finland

Richard A. JOHNSON
Senior Partner
Arnold & Porter
United States

Hiroshi KOJO
Engineer, Corporate Planning Divison
Honda Motor Co. Ltd
Japan

Staffan LARSSON
Director, Head of Analysis Division
NUTEK
Sweden

Hyung-Jong LEE
Deputy-Director
Economic Organization Division
Ministry of Foreign Affairs and Trade
Korea

Patrick LENAIN
Counsellor to the Head of Department
Economics Department
OECD

David LYON
Professor of Sociology and
Director, Surveillance Project
Queen's University
Canada

Yasuhisa MAEKAWA
Executive Vice President of Honda Motor Europe and
President of Honda R&D Europe
United Kingdom

Luigi MEZZANOTTE
CEO
LC Sistemia S.p.A.
Italy

Rudolf MÜLLER
Deputy Head of Directorate
State Secretariat for Economic Affairs (SECO)
Switzerland

Clive NORRIS
Professor
Department of Sociological Studies
University of Sheffield
United Kingdom

René OOSTERLINCK
Head, Navigation Department
European Space Agency (ESA)

Jean-Guy PAQUET
Président-Directeur général
Institut national d'optique, Quebec
Canada

Gerald QUIRCHMAYR
Professor of Computer and Information Science
University of Vienna, Austria and University of South Australia
and The Bob Hawke Prime Ministerial Centre
Australia

Herwig SCHLÖGL
Deputy Secretary-General
OECD

Nam-Niol SEO
Director, Crisis Management Center
National Security Council
Korea

Alfio TORRISI
Senior Executive Vice President
Strategic Planning and Budgetary Control
Istituto Poligrafico e Zecca dello Stato
(Stationery Office and Government Mint)
Italy

Frederik VON DEWALL
General Manager and Chief Economist
ING Group
Netherlands

OECD Secretariat

Advisory Unit to the Secretary-General

Barrie STEVENS
Deputy to the Director

Pierre-Alain SCHIEB
Counsellor
Head of Futures Project

Concetta MIANO
Assistant

Questionnaire on the quality of OECD publications

We would like to ensure that our publications meet your requirements in terms of presentation and editorial content. We would welcome your feedback and any comments you may have for improvement. Please take a few minutes to complete the following questionnaire. Answers should be given on a scale of 1 to 5 (1 = poor, 5 = excellent).

Fax or post your answer before 31 December 2004, and you will automatically be entered into the prize draw to **win a year's subscription to *OECD's Observer magazine.***

A. Presentation and layout

1. What do you think about the presentation and layout in terms of the following:

	Poor	Adequate		Excellent	
Readability (font, typeface)	1	2	3	4	5
Organisation of the book	1	2	3	4	5
Statistical tables	1	2	3	4	5
Graphs	1	2	3	4	5

B. Printing and binding

2. What do you think about the quality of the printed edition in terms of the following:

Quality of the printing	1	2	3	4	5
Quality of the paper	1	2	3	4	5
Type of binding	1	2	3	4	5

Not relevant, I am using the e-book ❏

3. Which delivery format do you prefer for publications in general?

Print ❏   CD ❏   E-book (PDF) via Internet ❏   Combination of formats ❏

C. Content

4. How accurate and up to date do you consider the content of this publication to be?

1   2   3   4   5

5. Are the chapter titles, headings and subheadings…

Clear   Yes ❏   No ❏
Meaningful   Yes ❏   No ❏

6. How do you rate the written style of the publication (*e.g.* language, syntax, grammar)?

1   2   3   4   5

D. General

7. Do you have any additional comments you would like to add about the publication?

....
....
....

Tell us who you are:

Name: ....   **E-mail:** ....

Fax: ....

Which of the following describes you?

IGO ❏   NGO ❏   Self-employed ❏   Student ❏
Academic ❏   Government official ❏   Politician ❏   Private sector ❏

Thank you for completing the questionnaire. Please fax your answers to: (33-1) 49 10 42 81 or mail it to the following address:
Questionnaire qualité PAC/PROD, Division des publications de l'OCDE
23, rue du Dôme – 92100 Boulogne Billancourt – France.

Title: The Emerging Security Economy – What Trade-offs in an open and mobile society

ISBN: 92-64-10772-X   **OECD Code (printed version):** 032004031P

---

* Please note: This offer is not open to OECD staff.

OECD PUBLICATIONS, 2, rue André-Pascal, 75775 PARIS CEDEX 16
PRINTED IN FRANCE
(03 2004 03 1 P) ISBN 92-64-10772-X – No. 53479 2004